EYEWITNESS *TRAVEL GUIDES*

SPANISH
PHRASE BOOK

D0767621

DORLING KINDERSLEY
LONDON • NEW YORK • STUTTGART • MOSCOW

A DORLING KINDERSLEY BOOK

Compiled by Lexus Ltd with Alicia de Benito de Harland and Mike Harland

Set in 9/9 Plantin and Plantin Light by Lexus Ltd
with Dittoprint Ltd, Glasgow
Printed in Great Britain by Cambus Litho

First published in Great Britain in 1997
by Dorling Kindersley Limited
9 Henrietta Street, London WC2E 8PS

Copyright 1997 © Dorling Kindersley Limited, London

A CIP catalogue record is available from the British Library.
ISBN 0-7513-1074-3

CONTENTS

PREFACE

This *Eyewitness Travel Guide Phrase Book* has been compiled by experts to meet the general needs of tourists and business travellers. Arranged under the headings of Hotels, Motoring and so forth, the ample selection of useful words and phrases is supported by a 2,000-line mini-dictionary. There is also an extensive menu guide listing approximately 600 dishes or methods of cooking and presentation.

Typical replies to questions you may ask during your journey, and the signs or instructions you may see or hear, are shown in tinted boxes. In the main text, the pronunciation of Spanish words and phrases is imitated in English sound syllables. The Introduction provides basic guidelines to Spanish pronunciation, and lists some key grammatical points to remember.

Eyewitness Travel Guides are recognized as the world's best travel guides. Each title features specially commissioned colour photographs, cutaways of major buildings, 3-D aerial views and detailed maps, plus information on sights, events, hotels, restaurants, shopping and entertainment.

Titles available in the series are:
Seville & Andalusia • Spain • London
France • Paris • Provence • Loire Valley
New York • San Francisco • Sydney • California
Rome • Venice & the Veneto • Florence & Tuscany • Italy
The Greek Islands • Greece: Athens & the Mainland
Vienna • Prague • Amsterdam
Great Britain • Ireland

INTRODUCTION

PRONUNCIATION

When reading the imitated pronunciation, stress that part which is underlined. Pronounce each syllable as if it formed part of an English word, and you will be understood sufficiently well. Remember the points below, and your pronunciation will be even closer to the correct Spanish. Use our audio-cassette of selected extracts from this book, and you should be word-perfect!

g   always hard as in 'get'

H   represents the guttural sound of 'ch' as in the Scottish 'loch' – *don't* pronounce this as 'lock'

I   pronounced as 'eye'

ow   as in 'cow'

s   always sound the Spanish 's' as a double 'ss' as in 'missing', *never* like the 's' in 'easy'

th   as in 'thin', *not* as in 'they'

y   always as in 'yet', *not* as in 'eye' (eg **bien** *byen*, **siento** *syentoh*)

Don't be worried by the varying pronunciations you are certain to hear in some parts of Spain, for example the sounding of 'z' (and of 'c' before e or i) like an English 's' ... although in this instance we recommend that you don't copy it, but lisp the sound as we have imitated it. Similarly, in certain circumstances, the Spanish 'v' can be pronounced as either a 'v' or a 'b' so that **vaca** sounds like 'baca' – as you'll hear in our recording.

GENDERS AND ARTICLES

Spanish has two genders for nouns – masculine and feminine. In this book, we generally give the definite article ('the') – **el** for masculine nouns, **la** for feminine nouns, **los** for masculine plural nouns and **las** for feminine plural nouns. Where the indefinite article ('a, an') is more appropriate, we have given **un** for masculine nouns and **una** for feminine nouns or the words for 'some', **unos** (masculine) and **unas** (feminine).

USEFUL EVERYDAY PHRASES

YES, NO, OK ETC

Yes/no
Sí/No
see/noh

Excellent!
¡Estupendo!
estoopendoh

Don't!
¡No!
noh

OK
Vale
baleh

That's fine
Está bien
esta byen

That's right
Eso es
essoh ess

GREETINGS, INTRODUCTIONS

How do you do? Pleased to meet you
¿Qué tal?, mucho gusto
keh tal, mootchoh goostoh

Good morning/good evening/good night
Buenos días/buenas tardes/buenas noches
bweh-noss dee-ass/bwehn-nass tardess/bweh-nass notchess

Goodbye/Bye
Adiós
ad-y__oss__

How are you? *(familiar)*
¿Cómo está usted? ¿Cómo estás?
k__oh__-moh est__a__ oost__eh__ *k__oh__-moh est__a__ss*

My name is ...
Me llamo ...
meh y__ah__-moh

What's your name? *(familiar)*
¿Cómo se llama usted? ¿Cómo te llamas?
k__oh__-moh seh y__ah__-ma oost__eh__ *k__oh__-moh teh y__ah__-mass*

What's his/her name?
¿Cómo se llama él/ella?
k__oh__-moh seh y__ah__-ma el/__eh__-ya

May I introduce ...?
Le presento a ...
leh pres__e__ntoh a

This is ... *(introducing a man/woman)*
Este/ésta es ...
__e__steh/__e__sta ess

Hello/Hi!
¡Hola!
__oh__-la

See you later!/Cheerio!
¡Hasta luego!
__a__sta lw__eh__-goh

It's been nice meeting you *(to a man/woman)*
Mucho gusto en conocerle/conocerla
m__oo__tchoh g__oo__stoh en konoh-th__ai__rleh/konoh-th__ai__rla

PLEASE, THANK YOU, APOLOGIES

Thank you/No thank you
Gracias/No, gracias
grath-yass/noh grath-yass

Please
Por favor
por fa-vor

Excuse me! *(when belching/sneezing etc)*
¡Perdón!
pair-don

Sorry!
¡Perdón!/Lo siento
pair-don/loh syentoh

I'm really sorry
Lo siento muchísimo
loh syentoh mootchee-seemoh

It was/wasn't my fault
Ha sido/no ha sido culpa mía
a seedoh/noh a seedoh koolpa mee-a

WHERE, HOW, ASKING

Excuse me please *(to get past)*
¿Me hace el favor?
meh ah-theh el fa-vor

Can you tell me ...?
¿Puede decirme ...?
pweh-deh detheer-meh

Can I have ...?
¿Me da ...?
meh da

Would you like a ...?
¿Quiere un/una ...?
ky_eh_-reh oon/_oo_na

Would you like to ...?
¿Le gustaría ...?
leh goostar_ce_-a

Is there ... here?
¿Hay ... aquí?
*I ... ak_ee_*

What's that?
¿Qué es eso?
keh ess _e_sso

Where can I get ...?
¿Dónde puedo conseguir ...?
d_o_ndeh p_weh_-doh konseh-_gee_r

How much is it?
¿Cuánto es?
kw_a_ntoh ess

Where is the ...?
¿Dónde está el/la ...?
d_o_ndeh est_a_ el/la

Where are the toilets?
¿Dónde están los servicios?
d_o_ndeh est_a_n loss sair-v_ee_th-yoss

ABOUT ONESELF

I'm from ...
Soy de ...
soy deh

I'm ... years old
Tengo ... años
teng-goh ... ahn-yoss

I'm a ...
Soy ...
soy

I'm married/divorced
Estoy casado/divorciado
estoy kasadoh/deevorss-yah-doh

I'm single
Soy soltero
soy soltairoh

I have ... sisters/brothers/children
Tengo ... hermanas/hermanos/hijos
teng-goh ... airmah-nass/airmah-noss/ee-Hoss

LIKES, DISLIKES, SOCIALIZING

I like/love ...
Me gusta/encanta el/la ...
meh goosta/enkanta el/la

I like/love swimming/travelling
Me gusta/encanta nadar/viajar
meh goosta/enkanta nadar/vya-Har

I don't like ...
No me gusta el/la ...
noh meh goosta el/la

10

I don't like swimming/travelling
No me gusta nadar/viajar
noh meh goosta nadar/vya-Har

I hate ...
Detesto ...
detestoh

Do you like ...?
¿Le gusta ...?
leh goosta

It's delicious/awful!
¡Es delicioso/horrible!
ess deleeth-yohsoh/orreebleh

I don't drink/smoke
No bebo/fumo
noh beboh/foomoh

Do you mind if I smoke?
¿Le importa que fume?
leh eemporta keh foomeh

I don't eat meat or fish
No como carne ni pescado
noh koh-moh karneh nee peskadoh

What would you like (to drink)?
¿Qué quiere (beber/tomar)?
keh kyeh-reh bebair/tomar

I would like a ...
Quería ...
keh-ree-a

Nothing for me thanks
No quiero nada, gracias
noh kyeh-roh nada grath-yass

I'll get this one
Ahora invito yo
a-ora eembeetoh yoh

Cheers!
¡Salud!
saloo

I would like to …
Quería …
keh-ree-a

Let's go to Seville/the cinema
Vamos a Sevilla/al cine
vamoss a sevee-ya/al theeneh

Let's go swimming/for a walk
Vamos a nadar/a dar un paseo
vamoss a nadar/a dar oon passeh-oh

What's the weather like?
¿Qué tiempo hace?
keh tyempoh ah-theh

The weather's awful
Hace un tiempo malísimo
ah-theh oon tyempoh maleesseemoh

It's pouring down
Está lloviendo a jarros
esta yovyendoh a Harross

It's really hot
Hace muchísimo calor
ah-theh mootcheesseemoh kalor

HELP, PROBLEMS

Can you help me?
¿Puede ayudarme?
pweh-deh ayoodarmeh

I don't understand
No comprendo
noh komprendoh

Do you speak English/French/German/?
¿Habla usted inglés/francés/alemán?
ah-bla oosteh eengless/franthess/alleh-man

Does anyone here speak English?
¿Alguien de aquí habla inglés?
algyen deh akee ahbla eengless

I can't speak Spanish
No hablo español
noh ah-bloh esspan-yoll

I don't know
No sé
noh seh

What's wrong?
¿Qué pasa?
keh passa

Please speak more slowly
Por favor, hable más despacio
por fa-vor ah-bleh mass desspath-yoh

Please write it down for me
Por favor, escríbamelo
por fa-vor eskreeba-meh-loh

I've lost my way
Me he perdido
meh eh pairdeedoh

Go away!
¡Lárguese!
largeh-seh

TALKING TO RECEPTIONISTS ETC

I have an appointment with ...
Tengo una cita con ...
teng-goh oona theeta kon

I'd like to see ...
Quisiera ver a ...
keess-yeh-ra vair a

Here's my card
Aquí tiene mi tarjeta
akee tyeneh mee tar-Heh-ta

My company is ...
Soy de la compañía ...
soy deh la kompanyee-a

May I use your phone?
¿Puedo usar su teléfono?
pweh-doh oossar soo teh-leffonoh

THINGS YOU'LL HEAR

¡adelante!	come in!
aquí tiene	here you are
¡bien!	good!
¡buen viaje!	have a good trip!

→

¿cómo?	pardon?
¿cómo está usted?	how are you?
¿cómo le va?	how are things?
¡cuánto lo siento!	I'm so sorry!
¡cuidado!	look out!
de nada	you're welcome, don't mention it
¿de verdad?	is that so?
¡encantado!	pleased to meet you!
eso es	that's right
exactamente/exacto	exactly
gracias, igualmente	thank you, the same to you
¡hasta luego!	cheerio!; see you later!
¡hola!	hello!, hi!
muchas gracias	thank you very much
muy bien, gracias	very well, thank you
– ¿y usted?	– and you?
no comprendo	I don't understand
no sé	I don't know
por favor	please
¿qué ha dicho?	what did you say?
¿qué tal?, mucho gusto	how do you do?, nice to meet you
sírvase usted mismo	help yourself
vale	OK

THINGS YOU'LL SEE

abierto	open
agua potable	drinking water
ascensor	lift
aseos	toilets
caballeros	gentlemen

→

15

caja	cashier, cash desk, till
calle	street
carretera	road
cerrado (por vacaciones)	closed (for holiday period)
día festivo	public holiday
empujar	push
entrada	way in, entrance
entrada gratis/libre	admission free
entre sin llamar	enter without knocking
festivos	bank holidays
horas de oficina	opening times
horas de visita	visiting hours
información turística	tourist information
laborables	working days
lavabos	toilets
ocupado	engaged
peligro	danger
planta baja	ground floor
precaución	caution
primer piso	first floor
privado	private
prohibido	prohibited, forbidden
recién pintado	wet paint
reservado	reserved
salida	way out
salida de emergencia	emergency exit
se alquila piso	flat to let
segundo piso	second floor
señoras	ladies
se prohíbe la entrada	no admittance
servicios	toilets
se vende	for sale
silencio	silence, quiet
sótano	basement
tirar	pull

COLLOQUIALISMS

You may hear these: to use some of them yourself could be risky!

agarrar un colocón	to get sozzled
a mares	loads
¡anda ya!	get away!, come off it!
cabrón	bastard
cacharro	thing, whatsit
¡cierra el pico!	shut your mouth!
cretino	moron
¡cuéntaselo a tu abuela!	pull the other one!
de pacotilla	rubbishy
¡Dios mío!	my God!, oh God!
¡eso sí que mola!	that's really terrific!
¡estupendo!	brilliant!
¡genial!	great!, fantastic!
ha sido una putada	it was a bloody nuisance
imbécil	nutter
ir de copas	to go on a pub crawl
la mar de …	ever so …
lo digo de cachondeo	I'm only joking
¡maldita sea!	damn!
me está tomando el pelo	you're pulling my leg
¡ni de coña!	not bloody likely!
¡no me da la (real) gana!	I'm damned if I will!
putada	dirty trick
¡qué barbaridad!	cor!
¡qué guai!	that's fantastic!
¿qué hay?	how's things?
¡qué va!	no way!
tía	bird
tío	bloke
¡vaya por Dios!	oh Christ!
¡váyase a paseo!	get lost!
¡vete a hacer puñetas!	bugger off!
ya está	there you are

DAYS, MONTHS, SEASONS

Sunday	domingo	*dom__ee__ngoh*
Monday	lunes	*l__oo__ness*
Tuesday	martes	*m__a__rtess*
Wednesday	miércoles	*my__ai__rkoh-less*
Thursday	jueves	*Hw__eh__-vess*
Friday	viernes	*vy__ai__rness*
Saturday	sábado	*s__a__bbadoh*

January	enero	*enn__eh__-roh*
February	febrero	*febr__eh__-roh*
March	marzo	*m__a__rthoh*
April	abril	*abr__ee__l*
May	mayo	*m__a__yyoh*
June	junio	*H__oo__n-yoh*
July	julio	*H__oo__l-yoh*
August	agosto	*ag__o__stoh*
September	septiembre	*set-y__e__mbreh*
October	octubre	*okt__oo__breh*
November	noviembre	*nov-y__e__mbreh*
December	diciembre	*deeth-y__e__mbreh*

Spring	primavera	*preema-v__eh__-ra*
Summer	verano	*ver__ah__-noh*
Autumn	otoño	*ot__o__n-yoh*
Winter	invierno	*eemb-y__ai__rnoh*

Christmas	Navidad	*navee-d__a__*
Christmas Eve	Nochebuena	*notcheh-bw__eh__-na*
Easter	Pascua,	*p__a__skwa,*
	Semana Santa	*sem__ah__-na s__a__nta*
Good Friday	Viernes Santo	*vy__ai__rness s__a__ntoh*
New Year	Año Nuevo	*__ah__n-yoh nw__eh__-voh*
New Year's Eve	Nochevieja	*notcheh-vy__eh__-Ha*

NUMBERS

0 cero *theh-roh*
1 uno, una* *oonoh, oona*
2 dos *doss*
3 tres *tress*
4 cuatro *kwatroh*
5 cinco *theenkoh*
6 seis *sayss*
7 siete *see-eh-teh*
8 ocho *otchoh*
9 nueve *nweh-veh*

10 diez *dyeth*
11 once *ontheh*
12 doce *doh-theh*
13 trece *treh-theh*
14 catorce *katortheh*
15 quince *keentheh*
16 dieciséis *dyeth-ee-sayss*
17 diecisiete *dyeth-ee-see-eh-teh*
18 dieciocho *dyeth-ee-otchoh*
19 diecinueve *dyeth-ee-nweh-veh*

20 veinte *vaynteh*
21 veintiuno *vayntee-oonoh*
22 veintidós *vayntee-doss*
30 treinta *traynta*
31 treinta y uno *trayntI oonoh*
32 treinta y dos *trayntI doss*
40 cuarenta *kwarenta*
50 cincuenta *theen-kwenta*
60 sesenta *sessenta*
70 setenta *setenta*
80 ochenta *otchenta*
90 noventa *noh-venta*
100 cien *thyen*
110 ciento diez *thyentoh dyeth*
200 doscientos, doscientas *doss-thyentoss, doss-thyentass*
500 quinientos, quinientas *keen-yentoss, keen-yentass*
700 setecientos, setecientas *seh-teh-thyentoss, seh-teh-thyentass*
1,000 mil *meel*
1,000,000 un millón *meel-yon*

* When **uno** precedes a masculine noun, it loses the final **o**, eg '1 point' is **un punto**. Feminine nouns take **una**, eg '1 peseta' **una peseta**. With numbers in the hundreds, 200, 300, 400 etc, the form ending in **-as** is used with feminine nouns, eg '300 notes' **trescientos billetes**; '500 pesetas' **quinientas pesetas**.

TIME

today	hoy	*oy*
yesterday	ayer	*ayyair*
tomorrow	mañana	*man-yah-na*
the day before yesterday	anteayer	*anteh-ayyair*
the day after tomorrow	pasado mañana	*passah-doh man-yah-na*
this week	esta semana	*esta semah-na*
next week	la semana que viene	*la semah-na keh vyeh-neh*
this morning	esta mañana	*esta man-yah-na*
this afternoon	esta tarde	*esta tardeh*
this evening	esta tarde/noche	*esta tardeh/notcheh*
tonight	esta noche	*esta notcheh*
yesterday afternoon	ayer por la tarde	*ayyair por la tardeh*
last night	anoche	*annotcheh*
tomorrow morning	mañana por la mañana	*man-yah-na por la man-yah-na*
tomorrow night	mañana por la noche	*man-yah-na por la notcheh*
in three days	dentro de tres días	*dentroh deh tress dee-ass*
three days ago	hace tres días	*ah-theh tress dee-ass*
late	tarde	*tardeh*
early	temprano	*temprah-noh*
soon	pronto	*prontoh*
later on	más tarde	*mass tardeh*
at the moment	en este momento	*en esteh momentoh*
second	un segundo	*segoondoh*
minute	un minuto	*meenootoh*
quarter of an hour	un cuarto de hora	*kwartoh deh ora*
half an hour	media hora	*meh-dya ora*

three quarters of an hour	tres cuartos de hora	*tress kwartoss deh ora*
hour	la hora	*ora*
day	el día	*dee-a*
every day	todos los días	*todoss loss dee-ass*
all day	todo el día	*todoh el dee-a*
the next day	al día siguiente	*al dee-a seegyenteh*
week	la semana	*semah-na*
fortnight, 2 weeks	la quincena	*keentheh-na*
month	el mes	*mess*
year	el año	*ahn-yoh*

TELLING THE TIME

The 24-hour clock is used more commonly than in Britain, both in the written form (as in timetables) and verbally (eg in enquiry offices). However, you will still hear the 12-hour clock used in everyday life.

'O'clock' is not normally translated in Spanish unless it is for emphasis, when **en punto** would be used. For example: **(es) la una (en punto)** is `(it's) one o'clock', whilst the plural form of the verb is used for all other hours, eg: **(son) las cinco (en punto)** is `(it's) five o'clock'.

The word 'past' is translated as **y** (='and'). In order to express minutes past the hour state the hour followed by **y** plus the number of minutes: so **las seis y diez** is 'ten past six'. The word 'to' is translated as **menos** (= 'less'). So, for example, **las diez menos veinte** is 'twenty to ten.' The word for 'quarter' is **cuarto**; so, **las siete menos cuarto** is 'quarter to seven' and **las cinco y cuarto** is 'quarter past five'. 'Half past' is expressed using **y media**, so **las seis y media** is 'half past six'.

The word 'at' is translated as **a** followed by **las**; for example, **a las tres y cuarto** is 'at quarter past three'. Remember, however, to change **las** to **la** when using 'one', thus 'at half past one' becomes **a la una y media**.

The expressions 'am' and 'pm' have no direct equivalents but the expressions **de la mañana** ('in the morning'), **de la tarde** (in the afternoon/evening – which extends up to 8 pm in Spain) and **de la noche** (at night – ie from 8 pm) are used to distinguish between times which might otherwise be confusing. For example, '6 am' is **las seis de la mañana** and '6 pm' is **las seis de la tarde**; '10 am' is **las diez de la mañana** and '10 pm' is **las diez de la noche**.

what time is it?	¿qué hora es?	*keh ora ess*
am	de la mañana	*deh la man-yah*
pm *(up to 8 pm)*	de la tarde	*deh la tardeh*
(from 8 pm)	de la noche	*deh la notcheh*
one o'clock	la una	*la oona*
ten past one	la una y diez	*la oona ee dyeth*
quarter past one	la una y cuarto	*la oona ee kwartoh*
half past one	la una y media	*la oona ee meh-dya*
twenty to two	las dos menos veinte	*lass doss meh-noss vaynteh*
quarter to two	las dos menos cuarto	*lass doss meh-noss kwartoh*
two o'clock	las dos (en punto)	*lass doss (en poontoh)*
13.00	las trece horas	*lass treh-theh orass*
16.30	las dieciséis treinta	*lass dyeth-ee-sayss traynta*
20.10	las veinte diez	*lass vaynteh dyeth*
at seven o'clock	a las siete	*a lass see-eh-teh*
noon	mediodía	*meh-dyoh dee-a*
midnight	medianoche	*meh-dya notcheh*

THE CALENDAR

The cardinal numbers on page 19 are used to express the date in Spanish. However, sometimes in formal Spanish, the ordinal number may be used instead, but only when used to express 'the first':

the first of May	el uno/el primero de mayo	*el oonoh/el preemeh-roh deh mayyoh*
the twentieth of June	el veinte de junio	*el vaynteh deh Hoon-yoh*

HOTELS

Hotels are divided into 5 classes (star rating), followed by the **pensiones** (guesthouses) which have three. Further down the scale come the **hotel-residencia** for longer stays and the **hostal** which is similar to a **pensión**. An **albergue** is usually a country hotel situated in a picturesque area and is meant for short stays. The previously state-run **paradores** are superior (often converted castles, palaces etc) and allow unlimited stays, though you will have to pay for the extra comfort and scenery. If travelling in high season it is always advisable to book accommodation in advance in the more popular areas.

USEFUL WORDS AND PHRASES

balcony	el balcón	*bal-kon*
bath *(tub)*	la bañera	*ban-yeh-ra*
bathroom	el cuarto de baño	*kwartoh deh bahn-yoh*
bed	la cama	*kah-ma*
bed and breakfast	alojamiento y desayuno	*aloh-Hamyentoh ee dessa-yoonoh*
bedroom	la habitación	*abbee-tath-yon*
bill	la cuenta	*kwenta*
breakfast	el desayuno	*dessa-yoonoh*
car park	el aparcamiento	*aparkamyentoh*
dining room	el comedor	*kommeh-dor*
dinner	la cena	*theh-na*
double bed	la cama doble, la cama de matrimonio	*kah-ma doh-bleh, kah-ma deh matreemonyoh*
double room	una habitación doble	*abbee-tath-yon doh-bleh*
foyer	el hall	*Hol*
full board	pensión completa	*penss-yon kompleh-ta*
guesthouse	la pensión	*penss-yon*
half board	media pensión	*meh-dya penss-yon*
hotel	el hotel	*oh-tell*

key	la llave	*yah-veh*
lift	el ascensor	*ass-then-sor*
lounge	el salón	*sa-lon*
lunch	la comida	*komee-da*
maid	la camarera	*kamareh-ra*
manager	el director	*deerek-tor*
receipt	la factura	*fak-toora*
reception	la recepción	*reh-thepth-yon*
receptionist	el recepcionista	*reh-thepth-yoneesta*
room	la habitación	*abbee-tath-yon*
room service	el servicio de habitaciones	*sairveeth-yoh deh abbeetath-yoh-ness*
shower	la ducha	*dootcha*
single bed	la cama individual	*kah-ma eendeeveed-wal*
single room	una habitación individual	*abbee-tath-yon eendeeveed-wal*
toilet	el wáter, el retrete	*vattair, retreh-teh*
twin room	una habitación con dos camas	*abbee-tath-yon kon doss kah-mass*
washbasin	el lavabo	*lavah-boh*

Have you any vacancies?
¿Tienen alguna habitación libre?
tyeh-nen algoona abbee-tath-yon leebreh

I have a reservation
He hecho una reserva
eh etchoh oona reh-sairva

I'd like a single room
Quería una habitación individual
keh-ree-a oona abbee-tath-yon eendeeveed-wal

I'd like a room with a balcony/bathroom
Quería una habitación con balcón/cuarto de baño
keh-ree-a oona abbee-tath-yon kon bal-kon/kwartoh deh bahn-yoh

I'd like a room for one night/three nights
Quería una habitación para una noche/para tres noches
keh-ree-a oona abbee-tath-yon parra oona notcheh/parra tress notchess

What is the charge per night?
¿Cuál es la tarifa por noche?
kwal ess la tarreefa por notcheh

I don't know yet how long I'll stay
Todavía no sé cuánto tiempo me voy a quedar
todavee-a noh seh kwantoh tyempoh meh voy a keh-dar

When is breakfast/dinner?
¿A qué hora es el desayuno/la cena?
a keh ora ess el dessa-yoonoh/la theh-na

Please wake me at 7 o'clock
Haga el favor de llamarme a las siete, ¿vale?
ah-ga el fa-vor deh yamar-meh a lass syeh-teh baleh

Can I have breakfast in my room?
¿Pueden servirme el desayuno en mi habitación?
pweh-den sair-veermeh el dessa-yoonoh en mee abbee-tath-yon

I'd like to have some laundry done
Quisiera utilizar el servicio de lavado
keess-yeh-ra ooteeleethar el sairveeth-yoh deh lavah-doh

I'll be back at 10 o'clock
Volveré a las diez
volveh-reh a lass dyeth

My room number is 205
El número de mi habitación es el doscientos cinco
el noomeh-roh deh mee abbee-tath-yon ess el dossthyentoss theenkoh

My booking was for a double room
Había reservado una habitación doble
abee-a resairvah-doh oona abbee-tath-yon doh-bleh

I asked for a room with an en-suite bathroom
Pedí una habitación con baño
peh-dee oona abbee-tath-yon kon bahn-yoh

The lamp is broken
La lámpara está rota
la lampara esta rohta

There is no toilet paper in the bathroom
No hay papel higiénico en el cuarto de baño
noh I papel ee-Hyeneekoh en el kwartoh deh bahn-yoh

The window won't open
No se puede abrir la ventana
noh seh pweh-deh abreer la ventah-na

There isn't any hot water
No hay agua caliente
noh I ahg-wa kalyenteh

The socket in the bathroom doesn't work
El enchufe del cuarto de baño no funciona
el entchoofeh del kwartoh deh bahn-yoh noh foonthyoh-na

I'm leaving tomorrow
Me marcho mañana
meh martchoh man-yah-na

When do I have to vacate the room?
¿A qué hora tengo que desocupar la habitación?
a keh ora teng-goh keh dessokoopar la abbee-tath-yon

Can I have the bill please?
¿Me da la cuenta, por favor?
meh da la kwenta por fa-vor

I'll pay by credit card
Pagaré con tarjeta (de crédito)
pagareh kon tar-Heh-ta deh kredeetoh

I'll pay cash
Pagaré al contado
pagareh al kontahdoh

Can you get me a taxi?
¿Puede llamar a un taxi?
pweh-deh yamar a oon taksee

Can you recommend another hotel?
¿Puede recomendarme otro hotel?
pweh-deh rekomendarmeh otroh oh-tell

THINGS YOU'LL SEE

acceso prohibido	staff only
albergue	country hotel
almuerzo	lunch
alojamiento y desayuno	bed and breakfast
aparcamiento	parking, car park
ascensor	lift
baño	bath
cena	dinner
CH	boarding house
comedor	dining room
comida	lunch, meal
completo	no vacancies
cuarto de baño	bathroom
cuenta	bill
desayuno	breakfast
ducha	shower
empujar	push
entrada	entrance
escaleras	stairs
habitación con dos camas	twin room
habitación doble	double room
habitación individual	single room
hotel-residencia	residential hotel

→

27

HR	residential hotel
media pensión	half board
parador	luxury hotel
pensión	guesthouse
pensión completa	full board
planta baja	ground floor
primer piso	first floor
prohibida la entrada	no admission
prohibido el paso	staff only
salida de emergencia	emergency exit
salón	lounge
servicio	toilet
solo para residentes	hotel patrons only
tirar	pull
wáter	toilet

REPLIES YOU MAY BE GIVEN

Lo siento, está lleno
I'm sorry, we're full

El hotel está completo
We have no vacancies

No nos quedan habitaciones individuales/dobles
There are no single/double rooms left

¿Para cuántas noches?
For how many nights?

¿Va a pagar al contado, o con tarjeta?
Will you be paying by cash or credit card?

Haga el favor de pagar por adelantado
Please pay in advance

Tiene que desocupar la habitación antes de las doce
You must vacate the room by midday

CAMPING AND CARAVANNING

There are plenty of recognized sites all over Spain, especially along the Mediterranean coast, and most are open all year round. Outside these sites you will need a permit from landowners or authorities such as the Forestry Authority – ask the Spanish Tourist office for details.

Youth hostels are open to members of the YHA, but in the high season it is best to book in advance and stays are limited to three nights – details from the Spanish Tourist Office in London or local offices in Spain.

USEFUL WORDS AND PHRASES

bucket	el cubo	_koo_-boh
campfire	una hoguera	oh-_geh_-ra
go camping	ir de camping	eer deh _kampeen_
campsite	un camping	_kampeen_
caravan	la caravana	karav_ah_-na
caravan site	un camping	_kampeen_
cooking utensils	los utensilios de cocina	ootens_eel_-yoss deh koth_ee_na
drinking water	agua potable	_ahg_-wa pott_ah_-bleh
ground sheet	la lona impermeable	_loh_-na eempair-meh-_ah_-bleh
hitchhike	hacer auto-stop	ath_air_ owtoh-st_op_
rope	una cuerda	kw_air_da
rubbish	la basura	bass_oo_ra
rucksack	la mochila	motch_ee_la
saucepans	las cazuelas	kath-w_eh_-lass
sleeping bag	el saco de dormir	s_ah_-koh deh dorm_eer_
tent	la tienda	t_yen_da
youth hostel	el albergue juvenil	alb_air_geh Hooven_eel_

Can I camp here?
¿Puedo acampar aquí?
pweh-doh akampar akee

Can we park the caravan here?
¿Podemos aparcar aquí la caravana?
podeh-moss apar-kar akee la karavah-na

Where is the nearest campsite/caravan site?
¿Dónde está el camping más cercano?
dondeh esta el kampeen mass thair-kah-noh

What is the charge per night?
¿Cuál es la tarifa por noche?
kwal ess la tarreefa por notcheh

How much is it for a week?
¿Cuánto es para una semana?
kwantoh ess parra oona sehmah-na

I only want to stay for one night
Es solo para una noche
ess soh-loh parra oona notcheh

We're leaving tomorrow
Nos vamos mañana
noss vah-moss manyah-na

Where is the kitchen?
¿Dónde está la cocina?
dondeh esta la kotheena

Can I light a fire here?
¿Puedo encender fuego aquí?
pweh-doh enthen-dair fweh-goh akee

Where can I get ...?
¿Dónde puedo conseguir ...?
dondeh pweh-doh konseh-geer

Is there any drinking water?
¿Hay agua potable aquí?
I ahg-wa pottah-bleh akee

THINGS YOU'LL SEE

agua	water
agua potable	drinking water
albergue juvenil	youth hostel
aseos	toilet, washroom
camping	campsite, caravan site
cocina	kitchen
duchas	showers
fuego	fire
luz	light
manta	blanket
no se admiten perros	no dogs allowed
precio	price
prohibido ...	no ...
prohibido acampar	no camping
prohibido el paso	no trespassing
prohibido encender fuego	no campfires
saco de dormir	sleeping bag
se alquila	for hire
se prohíbe ...	... forbidden
supermercado	supermarket
tarifa	charges
tienda	shop
uso	use
wáter	toilet

VILLAS AND APARTMENTS

You may be asked to pay for certain 'extras' not included in the original price. You might want to ask if electricity, gas etc is included. It's a good idea to ask about an inventory at the start, rather than be told something is missing later just as you are about to leave. You may be asked for a deposit – so make sure you get a receipt for this.

USEFUL WORDS AND PHRASES

agency	la agencia	*ah-Henthya*
bath	el baño	*bahn-yoh*
bathroom	el cuarto de baño	*kwartoh deh bahn-yoh*
bedroom	el dormitorio	*dormee-tor-yoh*
blind	la persiana	*perss-yahna*
blocked	atascado	*atass-kah-doh*
boiler	la caldera	*kaldeh-ra*
break	romper	*rompair*
broken	roto	*rohtoh*
caretaker	el encargado,	*enkargah-doh,*
	el portero	*porteh-roh*
central heating	la calefacción central	*kaleffakthyon thentral*
cleaner	la señora de la	*sen-yora deh la*
	limpieza	*leempyeh-tha*
cooker	la cocina	*kotheena*
deposit	el depósito	*deh-posseetoh*
drain	el desagüe	*desahg-weh*
dustbin	(el cubo de) la basura	*kooboh deh la bassoora*
duvet	el edredón	*edreh-don*
electrician	un electricista	*elektreetheesta*
electricity	la electricidad	*elektreetheedad*
fridge	la nevera	*neh-veh-ra*
fusebox	la caja de fusibles	*kah-Ha deh fooseebless*
gas	el gas	*gas*
grill	la parrilla, el grill	*parree-ya, greell*
heater	la estufa	*estoofa*

32

iron	la plancha	*pl<u>a</u>ntcha*
ironing board	la tabla de planchar	*t<u>a</u>h-bla deh plantch<u>a</u>r*
key(s)	la(s) llave(s)	*la(ss) y<u>a</u>hveh(ss)*
kitchen	la cocina	*koth<u>ee</u>na*
leak *(in roof)*	una gotera	*goht<u>eh</u>-ra*
(in pipe)	un agujero	*ahgoo-H<u>eh</u>-roh*
light	la luz	*looth*
light bulb	la bombilla	*bomb<u>ee</u>-ya*
living room	el cuarto de estar	*kw<u>a</u>rtoh deh est<u>a</u>r*
maid	la sirvienta	*seerv<u>ye</u>nta*
pillow	la almohada	*almoh-<u>a</u>hda*
pillow slip	la funda de almohada	*f<u>oo</u>nda deh almoh-<u>a</u>hda*
plumber	un fontanero	*fontan<u>eh</u>-roh*
refund	un reembolso	*reh-emb<u>o</u>lsoh*
sheets	las sábanas	*s<u>a</u>hbanass*
shower	la ducha	*d<u>oo</u>tcha*
sink	el fregadero	*fregad<u>eh</u>-roh*
stopcock	la llave de paso	*y<u>a</u>h-veh deh p<u>a</u>h-soh*
swimming pool	la piscina	*peessth<u>ee</u>-na*
swimming pool engineer	el encargado de la piscina	*enkarg<u>a</u>h-doh deh la peessth<u>ee</u>-na*
tap	un grifo	*gr<u>ee</u>foh*
toilet	el retrete, el wáter	*retr<u>eh</u>-teh, v<u>a</u>ttair*
towel	la toalla	*toh-<u>ay</u>-a*
washing machine	la lavadora	*lavad<u>o</u>ra*
water	el agua	*<u>ah</u>g-wa*
water heater	el calentador (del agua)	*kalentad<u>o</u>r del <u>ah</u>g-wa*

Does the price include electricity/cleaning?
¿Está la electricidad/la limpieza incluída?
est<u>a</u> la elektreethee<u>a</u>d/la leempy<u>eh</u>-tha eenklw<u>ee</u>da

Do I need to sign an inventory?
¿Hará falta que firme algún inventario?
ar<u>a</u> f<u>a</u>lta keh f<u>ee</u>rmeh alg<u>oo</u>n eembent<u>a</u>ryoh

Where is this item?
¿Dónde está este artículo?
dondeh esta esteh arteekooloh

Please take it off the inventory
Haga el favor de quitarlo del inventario
ah-ga el fa-vor deh keetarloh del eembentaryoh

We've broken this
Se nos ha roto esto
seh noss a rohtoh estoh

This was broken when we arrived
Esto estaba roto cuando llegamos
estoh estah-ba rohtoh kwandoh yehgah-moss

This was missing when we arrived
Esto faltaba cuando llegamos
estoh faltah-ba kwandoh yehgah-moss

Can I have my deposit back?
¿Me devuelve el depósito?
meh deh-vwelveh el deh-posseetoh

Can we have an extra bed?
¿Puede ponernos otra cama más?
pweh-deh ponairnoss otra kah-ma mass

Can we have more crockery/cutlery?
¿Puede ponernos más platos y vasos/cubiertos?
pweh-deh ponairnoss mass plah-toss ee vah-soss/koob-yairtoss

Where is ...?
¿Dónde está ...?
dondeh esta

When does the maid come?
¿Cuándo viene la sirvienta?
kwandoh vyeh-neh la seervyenta

34

Where can I buy/find ...?
¿Dónde podría comprar/encontrar ...?
dondeh podree-a komprar/enkontrar

How does the water heater work?
¿Cómo funciona el calentador (de agua)?
koh-moh foonthyoh-na el kalentador deh ahg-wa

Do you do ironing/baby-sitting?
¿Hace usted la plancha/cuida usted niños?
ah-theh oosteh la plantcha/kweeda oosteh neenyoss

Do you prepare lunch/dinner?
¿Prepara usted la comida/la cena?
prepah-ra oosteh la komee-da/la theh-na

Do we have to pay extra or is it included?
¿Hay que pagar aparte o está incluído en el precio?
I keh pagar aparteh oh esta eenklweedoh en el prethyoh

The shower doesn't work
No funciona la ducha
noh foonthyoh-na la dootcha

The sink is blocked
El fregadero está atascado
el fregadeh-roh esta ataskah-doh

The sink/toilet is leaking
El fregadero/retrete se sale
el fregadeh-roh/retreh-teh seh sah-leh

There's a burst pipe
Hay una cañería rota
I oona kan-yeree-a rohta

The roof leaks
Hay una gotera en el tejado
I oona gohteh-ra en el teh-Hah-doh

The tank leaks
Hay un agujero en el depósito
I oon ahgoo-Heh-roh en el deposseetoh

There's a gas leak
El gas se está saliendo
el gas seh esta salyendoh

The rubbish has not been collected for three days
Llevan tres días sin recoger la basura
yeh-van tress dee-ass seen rekoh-Hair la bassoora

There's no electricity/gas/water
No hay luz/gas/agua
noh I looth/gas/ahg-wa

The bottled gas has run out – how do we get a new cylinder?
Se ha acabado el butano – ¿cómo podemos conseguir otra bombona?
seh ah akabah-doh el bootah-noh – koh-moh podeh-moss konsegeer oh-tra bomboh-na

Can you mend it today?
¿Puede arreglarlo hoy?
pweh-deh arreglarlo oy

Send your bill to ...
Mande la factura a ...
mandeh la faktoora a

I'm staying at ...
Estoy en ...
estoy en

Thanks for looking after us so well
Gracias por tratarnos tan bien
grath-yass por tratarnoss tam byen

See you again next year
Hasta el año que viene
asta el ahn-yoh keh vyeh-neh

MOTORING

Spanish motorways (**autopistas**) can be expensive to use because of the tolls. The best roads to use are the national main roads (**nacionales**), as they often have crawler-lanes for heavy vehicles, especially on gradients, which makes overtaking much easier. In recent years, however, many dual carriageways (**autovías**) have been built. Secondary roads, **comarcales**, are not so good and can often be in quite poor condition.

The rule of the road is drive on the right, overtake on the left. Secondary roads give way to major routes at junctions and crossroads. In the case of roads having equal status, or at unmarked junctions, traffic coming from the **RIGHT** has priority. Look out for the pictorial signs for priority on narrow bridges etc. A system worth noting for changing direction or for crossing over dual carriageways is a semi-circular slip road which is usually signposted **cambio de sentido**.

The speed limit on the **nacionales** is 100 km/h (62 mph) and on the **autopistas** and **autovías** it's 120km/h (75 mph); otherwise keep to the speed shown. In built-up areas the limit will vary between 40 km/h and 60 km/h (25-35 mph). Equipment to be carried at all times includes a spare set of bulbs and a red triangle in case of breakdown or accidents. The Traffic Police patrols, **Guardia Civil de Tráfico**, will help you if in trouble, just as they will be ready to fine you on the spot should you infringe the law!

Petrol stations on the main roads are usually open 24 hours a day. They are seldom self-service. Unleaded petrol is not readily available outside cities and main tourist areas. Fuel ratings are as follows: **normal** 2-star, **super** 3-star, **extra** 4-star, **gas-oil** diesel, **sin plomo** unleaded.

Parking in Spain is generally less restrictive – look out for the signs as there are no markings on the kerb. In main towns and cities, however, the central area will come under what is often known as the **zona azul** with only restricted parking allowed – look out for parking meters or the more common 'pay and display' points. Alternatively, there are more and more underground car parks which operate on a ticket and barrier system.

SOME COMMON ROAD SIGNS

aduana	customs
apagar luces de cruce	headlights off
aparcamiento	car park
atención al tren	beware of trains
autopista	motorway
autopista de peaje	motorway with toll
callejón sin salida	no thoroughfare
calle peatonal	pedestrian precinct
calzada deteriorada	bad surface
calzada irregular	uneven surface
cambio de sentido	junction
carretera cortada	road closed
ceda el paso	give way
centro ciudad	town centre
centro urbano	town centre
circule despacio	slow
circunvalación	ring road
cruce	crossroads
desvío	diversion
desvío provisional	temporary diversion
encender luces de cruce	headlights on
escalón lateral	no hard shoulder
escuela	school
final de autopista	end of motorway
firme en mal estado	bad surface
hielo	black ice
información turística	tourist information
obras	roadworks
ojo al tren	beware of trains
paso a nivel	level crossing
paso subterráneo	pedestrian underpass
peaje	toll
peatón, circula por tu izquierda	pedestrians, keep to the left

→

peatones	pedestrians
peligro	danger
peligro deslizamientos	slippery road surface
precaución	caution
prohibido aparcar	no parking
prohibido el paso	no trespassing
puesto de socorro	first aid
salida de camiones	works exit
vado permanente	in constant use *(no parking)*
vehículos pesados	heavy vehicles
velocidad controlada por radar	automatic speed monitor
zona azul	restricted parking zone
zona de estacionamento limitado	restricted parking area

USEFUL WORDS AND PHRASES

automatic	automático	*owtoh-mateekoh*
bonnet	el capó	*kapo*
boot	el maletero	*malleh-teh-roh*
brake	el freno	*freh-noh*
breakdown	una avería	*avveh-ree-a*
car	el coche	*kotcheh*
caravan	la caravana	*karra-vah-na*
car park	el aparcamiento	*aparkamyento*
clutch	el embrague	*embrah-geh*
crossroads	el cruce	*kroo-theh*
drive	conducir	*kondoo-theer*
driving licence	el permiso/	*pairmeesso/*
	el carnet	*karneh*
	de conducir	*deh kondoo-theer*
engine	el motor	*moh-tor*
exhaust	el tubo de escape	*tooboh deh eskah-peh*
fanbelt	la correa del	*korreh-a del*
	ventilador	*venteela-dor*

garage *(repairs)*	un taller, un garaje	*tayair, garah-Heh*
(for petrol)	una gasolinera	*gassoh-leeneh-ra*
gear	la marcha	*martcha*
gear box	la caja de velocidades	*kah-Ha deh velotheedah-dess*
gears	las marchas	*mar-tchass*
headlights	las luces de cruce	*loothess deh kroo-theh*
indicator	el intermitente	*eentairmeetenteh*
junction	el cruce	*kroo-theh*
(motorway entry)	un enlace de entrada	*enlah-theh deh entrah-da*
(motorway exit)	un enlace de salida	*enlah-theh deh saleeda*
lorry	el camión	*kam-yon*
manual	manual	*man-wal*
mirror	el (espejo) retrovisor	*esspeh-Hoh retroh-veessor*
motorbike	la moto(cicleta)	*motoh-thee-kleh-ta*
motorway	la autopista	*owtoh-peesta*
number plate	la matrícula	*matree-koola*
petrol	la gasolina	*gassoh-leena*
petrol station	una gasolinera	*gassoh-leeneh-ra*
rear lights	las luces traseras	*loothess trasseh-rass*
road	la carretera	*karreh-teh-ra*
spares	los repuestos	*reh-pwestoss*
spark plug	la bujía	*boo-Hee-a*
speed	la velocidad	*velothee-da*
speed limit	el límite de velocidad	*leemeeteh deh velothee-da*
speedometer	el cuentakilómetros	*kwenta-keelomeh-tross*
steering wheel	el volante	*voh-lanteh*
tow	remolcar	*reh-molkar*
traffic lights	el semáforo	*seh-mafforoh*
trailer	el remolque	*reh-molkeh*
tyre	el neumático	*neh-oo-mateekoh*
van	la furgoneta	*foorgoneh-ta*
wheel	la rueda	*rweh-da*
windscreen	el parabrisas	*para-bree-sass*
windscreen wiper	el limpiaparabrisas	*leempya-parabreessass*

I'd like some petrol/oil/water
Quería gasolina/aceite/agua
keh-ree-a gassoh-leena/athay-teh/ahg-wa

Fill her up please!
¡Lleno, por favor!
yeh-noh por fa-vor

35 litres of 4-star please
Póngame treinta y cinco litros de extra
ponga-meh traynti theenkoh leetross deh extra

Would you check the tyres please?
¿Podría revisar los neumáticos, por favor?
podree-a revee-sarmeh loss neh-oo-mateekoss por fa-vor

Do you do repairs?
¿Hacen reparaciones?
ah-then reparrath-yoh-ness

Can you repair the clutch?
¿Pueden arreglarme el embrague?
pweh-den arreh-glarmeh el embrah-geh

There is something wrong with the engine
Hay algo que no va bien en el motor
i algoh keh noh va byen en el moh-tor

The engine is overheating
El motor se calienta demasiado
el moh-tor seh kal-yenta deh-massyah-doh

I need a new tyre
Necesito un neumático nuevo
neh-thessee-toh oon neh-oo-matikoh nweh-voh

Can you replace this?
¿Pueden cambiarme esto?
pwehden kambyarmeh estoh

The indicator is not working
El intermitente no funciona
el eentairmeetenteh noh foonthyoh-na

How long will it take?
¿Cuánto tiempo tardarán?
kwantoh tyempoh tardaran

I'd like to hire a car
Quería alquilar un coche
keh-ree-a alkee-lar oon kotcheh

I'd like an automatic/a manual
Quiero un coche automático/manual
kyeroh oon kotcheh owtoh-mateekoh/man-wal

How much is it for one day?
¿Cuánto cuesta para un día?
kwantoh kwesta parra oon dee-a

Is there a mileage charge?
¿Tiene suplemento por kilómetro?
tyeh-neh sooplementoh por keelometroh

When do I have to return it?
¿Cuándo tengo que devolverlo?
kwandoh teng-goh keh devolvairloh

Where is the nearest garage? *(for repairs)*
¿Dónde está el taller más cercano?
dondeh esta el tayair mass thair-kah-noh

(for petrol)
¿Dónde está la gasolinera más cercana?
dondeh esta la gassoh-leeneh-ra mass thair-kah-na

Where can I park?
¿Dónde puedo aparcar?
dondeh pweh-doh affpar-kar

Can I park here?
¿Puedo aparcar aquí?
pweh-doh appar-kar akee

How do I get to Seville?
¿Cómo se va a Sevilla?
koh-moh seh va a sevee-ya

Is this the road to Malaga?
¿Es ésta la carretera de Málaga?
ess esta la karreh-teh-ra deh malaga

Which is the quickest way to Madrid?
¿Cuál es el camino más rápido para Madrid?
kwal ess el kameenoh mass rapeedoh parra madreed

DIRECTIONS YOU MAY BE GIVEN

a la derecha/izquierda	on the right/left
después de pasar el/la ...	go past the ...
la primera a la derecha	first on the right
la segunda a la izquierda	second on the left
todo derecho	straight on
tuerza a la derecha	turn right
tuerza a la izquierda	turn left

THINGS YOU'LL SEE

aceite	oil
agua	water
aire	air
apague el motor	switch off engine
aparcamiento subterráneo	underground car park
área de servicios	service area, motorway services
cola	queue →

completo	car park full
(cubitos de) hielo	ice cubes
entrada	way in
estación de servicio	service station
extra	4-star
garaje	garage
gas-oil	diesel
gasolina	petrol, fuel
gasolinera	filling station
introduzca el dinero exacto	exact change
nivel del aceite	oil level
normal	2-star
presión	air pressure
presión de los neumáticos	tyre pressure
prohibido fumar	no smoking
recoja su ticket	take a ticket
reparación	repairs
salida	exit
sin plomo	unleaded
solo para residentes del hotel	hotel patrons only
super	3-star
taller (de reparaciones)	garage
(tren de) lavado automático	car wash

THINGS YOU'LL HEAR

¿Lo quiere automático o manual?
Would you like an automatic or a manual?

Su permiso/carnet de conducir, por favor
May I see your driving licence?

Su pasaporte, por favor
Your passport, please

TRAVELLING AROUND

AIR TRAVEL

Numerous international airlines provide services to Spanish destinations including: Madrid, Barcelona, Bilbao, Valencia, Alicante, Malaga, Seville, Santiago, Tenerife and Las Palmas in the Canaries, and Palma, Menorca and Ibiza in the Balearic Islands. There is also a domestic network connecting the main cities in Spain.

RAIL TRAVEL

The Spanish national railway system is called **RENFE** (*ren-fay*). Most trains are slow when compared to long-distance buses, even between major cities, but they are reasonably comfortable and inexpensive. The main types of train are:

AVE	High-speed train covering the Madrid – Seville line.
TALGO, TER	Fast diesel trains with air-conditioning; a supplement is required in addition to the normal fare. The **TALGO** is much more luxurious than the **TER**.
TAF	Slower diesel train used on secondary routes.
Exprés	A misleading name, as this is a slow night train stopping at all stations.
Rápido	Also misleading as it is just a daytime version of the **exprés**.
Automotor **Cercanías** **Ferrobús** **Omnibús** }	Local short-distance trains.

LONG-DISTANCE BUS TRAVEL

There is an excellent coach network covering the whole of Spain, giving a better connecting service between cities and covering the gaps in the railway system. The coaches are comfortable and fast, and have facilities such as video and air-conditioning.

LOCAL BUSES

All Spanish cities have a good bus network. Most buses are one-man operated and you pay the driver as you enter. Since there is generally a flat fare, it is cheaper to buy a book of tickets called a **bonobús** and there are also other types of runabout ticket.

UNDERGROUND

Both Madrid and Barcelona have an underground system, the **metro**. Again, a flat fare is in operation and you can buy a **taco** (book of tickets) or a 7-day ticket giving unlimited travel.

TAXI AND BOAT, OTHER TRANSPORT

There is a daily boat service to the Balearics (usually overnight) and a less frequent service to the Canaries, taking about two days. There is also a daily ferry linking Algeciras to North African ports such as Tangiers, Ceuta and Melilla.

Taxis display a green light at night, and a sign in the windscreen says if they are for hire (**libre**).

USEFUL WORDS AND PHRASES

adult	un adulto	*ad<u>oo</u>l-toh*
airport	el aeropuerto	*ah-airoh-pw<u>ai</u>r-toh*
airport bus	el autobús del aeropuerto	*owtoh-<u>boo</u>ss del ah-airoh-pw<u>ai</u>r-toh*
aisle seat	un asiento de pasillo	*ass-y<u>e</u>ntoh deh pass<u>ee</u>-yoh*
baggage claim	la recogida de equipajes	*rekoh-H<u>ee</u>da deh ekee-p<u>ah</u>-Hess*
boarding card	la tarjeta de embarque	*tar-H<u>e</u>h-ta deh emb<u>a</u>r-keh*
boat	el barco	*b<u>a</u>rkoh*

booking office	el despacho de billetes	*dess-patchoh deh bee-yeh-tess*
buffet	la cafetería	*kaffeh-teh-ree-a*
bus	el autobús	*owtoh-booss*
bus station	la estación de autobuses	*estath-yon deh owtoh-boossess*
bus stop	la parada del autobús	*parah-da del owtoh-booss*
carriage	el vagón	*va-gon*
check-in desk	el mostrador de facturación	*mostra-dor deh faktoorath-yon*
child	un niño/una niña	*neen-yoh/neen-yah*
coach *(bus)*	el autocar	*owtoh-kar*
compartment	el compartimento	*kompartee-mentoh*
connection	un enlace	*enlah-theh*
cruise	un crucero	*krootheh-roh*
currency exchange	el cambio de moneda	*kamb-yoh deh monneh-da*
customs	Aduana	*ad-wah-na*
departure lounge	salidas	*salee-dass*
domestic	nacional	*nath-yonal*
driver	el conductor	*kondook-tor*
emergency exit	la salida de emergencia	*salee-da deh eh-mair-Henth-ya*
entrance	la entrada	*entrah-da*
exit	la salida	*salee-da*
fare	el billete	*bee-yeh-teh*
ferry	el ferry	*ferree*
first class	primera (clase)	*preemeh-ra klah-seh*
flight	el vuelo	*vweh-loh*
flight number	el número de vuelo	*noomeh-roh deh vweh-loh*
gate	la puerta (de embarque)	*pwair-ta deh embar-keh*
international	internacional	*eentairnath-yonal*
left-luggage office	la consigna	*konseeg-na*

47

lost property office	la oficina de objetos perdidos	*offee-theena deh ob-Heh-toss pairdee-doss*
luggage trolley	un carrito para el equipaje	*karree-toh parra ekee-pah-Heh*
network map	un plano	*plah-noh*
non-smoking	no fumadores	*noh fooma-doress*
number 5 bus	el (autobús número) cinco	*owtoh-booss noomeh-roh theenkoh*
passport	el pasaporte	*passa-porteh*
platform	el andén	*an-den*
port	el puerto	*pwair-toh*
quay	el muelle	*mweh-yeh*
railway	el ferrocarril	*ferroh-karreel*
reserved seat	un asiento reservado	*ass-yentoh reh-sair-vah-doh*
restaurant car	el vagón-restaurante	*va-gon restow-ranteh*
return ticket	un billete de ida y vuelta	*bee-yeh-teh deh eeda ee vwel-ta*
seat	un asiento	*ass-yentoh*
second class	segunda (clase)	*segoonda klah-seh*
single ticket	un billete de ida	*bee-yeh-teh deh eeda*
sleeper	el coche-cama	*kotcheh kah-ma*
smoking	fumadores	*fooma-doress*
station	la estación	*estath-yon*
subway	paso subterráneo	*passoh soob-terrah-neh-oh*
taxi	un taxi	*taksee*
terminus *(bus)*	la terminal	*tairmee-nal*
(underground)	la estación terminal	*estath-yon tairmee-nal*
ticket	un billete	*bee-yeh-teh*
timetable	el horario	*oh-rar-yoh*
train	el tren	*tren*
underground	el metro	*meh-troh*
waiting room	la sala de espera	*sah-la deh espeh-ra*
window seat	un asiento de ventanilla	*ass-yentoh deh ventanee-ya*

AIR TRAVEL

A non-smoking seat please
Un asiento en la sección de no fumadores, por favor
oon ass-yentoh en la sekth-yon deh noh fooma-doress por fa-vor

I'd like a window seat please
Quería un asiento junto a la ventanilla, por favor
keh-ree-a oon ass-yentoh Hoontoh a la ventanee-ya por fa-vor

How long will the flight be delayed?
¿Cuánto retraso lleva el vuelo?
kwantoh reh-trah-soh yeh-va el vweh-loh

Which gate for the flight to Seville?
¿Cuál es la puerta de embarque para el vuelo de Sevilla?
kwal ess la pwair-ta deh embar-keh parra el vweh-loh deh sev-ee-ya

RAIL, BUS AND UNDERGROUND TRAVEL

When does the train/bus for Cadiz leave?
¿A qué hora sale el tren/autobús para Cádiz?
a keh ora sah-leh el tren/owtoh-booss parra kah-deeth

When does the train/bus from Barcelona arrive?
¿A qué hora llega el tren/autobús de Barcelona?
a keh ora yeh-ga el tren/owtoh-booss deh bartheh-loh-na

When is the next train/bus to Alicante?
¿A qué hora sale el próximo tren/autobús para Alicante?
a keh ora sah-leh el prok-seemoh tren/owtoh-booss parra aleekanteh

When is the first/last train/bus to Saragossa?
¿A qué hora sale el primer/último tren/autobús para Zaragoza?
a keh ora sah-leh el preemair/ool-teemoh tren/owtoh-booss parra tharagoh-tha

'hat is the fare to Granada?
¿Cuánto es el billete para Granada?
kwantoh ess el bee-yeh-teh parra granahda

Do I have to pay a supplement?
¿Tengo que pagar suplemento?
teng-goh keh pagar soopleh-mentoh

Do I have to change?
¿Tengo que hacer transbordo?
teng-goh keh athair tranz-bordoh

Does the train/bus stop at Salamanca?
¿Para el tren/autobús en Salamanca?
pah-ra el tren/owtoh-booss en salamanka

How long does it take to get to Cordoba?
¿Cuánto tiempo se tarda en llegar a Córdoba?
kwantoh tyempoh seh tar-da en yeh-gar a kordohba

Where can I buy a ticket?
¿Dónde puedo sacar un billete?
dondeh pweh-doh sakar oon bee-yeh-teh

REPLIES YOU MAY BE GIVEN

El próximo tren sale a las dieciocho horas
The next train leaves at 1800 hours

Haga transbordo en Salamanca
Change at Salamanca

Tiene que pagar suplemento
You must pay a supplement

Ya no quedan asientos para Madrid
There are no more seats available for Madrid

A single/return ticket to Gerona, please
Un billete de ida/de ida y vuelta a Gerona, por favor
oon bee-yeh-teh deh eeda/deh eeda ee vwel-ta a Herrohna por fa-vor

Could you help me get a ticket?
¿Podría usted ayudarme a sacar un billete?
podree-a oosteh ayoo-darmeh a sakar oon bee-yeh-teh

I'd like to reserve a seat
Quería reservar un asiento
keh-ree-a reh-sair-var oon ass-yentoh

Is this the right train/bus for Almeria?
¿Es éste el tren/autobús para Almería?
ess esteh el tren/owtoh-booss parra almeh-ree-a

Is this the right platform for the Seville train?
¿Es éste el andén para el tren de Sevilla?
ess esteh el an-den parra el tren deh sev-ee-ya

Which platform for the Granada train?
¿Qué andén para el tren de Granada?
keh an-den parra el tren deh granahda

Is the train/bus late?
¿Lleva retraso el tren/autobús?
yeh-va reh-trah-soh el tren/owtoh-booss

Could you help me with my luggage please?
¿Puede ayudarme con estas maletas, por favor?
pweh-deh ayoodar-meh kon estass maleh-tas por fa-vor

Is this a non-smoking compartment?
¿Está prohibido fumar aquí?
esta pro-ee-beedoh foomar akee

Is this seat free?
¿Está libre este asiento?
esta leebreh esteh ass-yentoh

This seat is taken
Este asiento está ocupado
esteh ass-yentoh esta okoopah-doh

I have reserved this seat
Tengo reservado este asiento
teng-goh reh-sair-vah-doh esteh ass-yentoh

May I open/close the window?
¿Puedo abrir/cerrar la ventana?
pweh-doh abreer/therrar la ventah-na

When do we arrive in Bilbao?
¿A qué hora llegamos a Bilbao?
a keh ora yeh-gah-moss a beelbah-oh

What station is this?
¿Qué estación es ésta?
keh estath-yon ess esta

Do we stop at Aranjuez?
¿Paramos en Aranjuez?
parah-moss en aran-Hweth

Would you keep an eye on my things for a moment?
¿Podría usted guardarme las cosas un momento?
podree-a ooss-teh gwar-darmeh lass koh-sass oon momentoh

Is there a restaurant car on this train?
¿Lleva vagón-restaurante este tren?
yeh-va va-gon restow-ranteh esteh tren

Where is the nearest underground station?
¿Dónde está la estación de metro más cercana?
dondeh esta la estath-yon deh meh-troh mass thair-kah-na

Where is there a bus stop?
¿Dónde hay una parada de autobús?
dondeh I oona parah-da deh owtoh-booss

Which buses go to Merida?
¿Qué autobuses van a Mérida?
keh owtoh-boossess van a meh-reeda

How often do the buses to Madrid run?
¿Cada cuánto tiempo pasan los autobuses para Madrid?
kah-da kwantoh tyempoh pah-san loss owtoh-boossess parra madree

Will you let me know when we're there?
¿Puede avisarme cuando lleguemos?
pweh-deh aveess-armeh kwandoh yeh-geh-moss

Do I have to get off yet?
¿Tengo que bajarme ya?
teng-goh keh ba-Harmeh ya

How do you get to Nerja?
¿Cómo se va a Nerja?
koh-moh seh va a nair-Ha

Do you go near San Pedro?
¿Pasa usted cerca de San Pedro?
pah-sa oosteh thair-ka deh san peh-droh

TAXI AND BOAT

Where can I get a taxi?
¿Dónde puedo tomar un taxi?
dondeh pweh-doh tomar oon taksee

I want to go to ...
Quiero ir a ...
kee-eh-roh eer a

Can you let me off here?
Pare aquí, por favor
pah-reh akee por fa-vor

How much is it to El Escorial?
¿Cuánto cuesta ir a El Escorial?
kwantoh kwesta eer a el eskoree-al

Could you wait here for me and take me back?
¿Puede esperarme aquí y llevarme de vuelta?
pweh-deh espeh-rar-meh akee ee yeh-var-meh deh vwelta

Where can I get a ferry to Palma?
¿Dónde se puede coger un ferry para Palma?
dondeh seh pweh-deh koh-Hair oon ferree parra palma

THINGS YOU'LL SEE

abstenerse de fumar	no smoking please
Aduana	customs
adultos	adults
a los andenes	to the trains
andén	platform
asientos	seats
automotor	local short-distance train
AVE	high-speed train
billete/billetes	ticket/tickets, ticket office
billete de andén	platform ticket
bocadillos	sandwiches, snacks
bonobús	book of 10 bus tickets
cambio de moneda	currency exchange
coche-cama	sleeper
consigna	left-luggage office
control de pasaportes	passport control
demora	delay
Días Azules	cheap travel days
domingos y festivos	Sundays and public holidays
entrada	entrance
entrada por delante/por detrás	entry at the front/rear

→

equipajes	left-luggage office
escala	intermediate stop
estación principal	central station
excepto domingos	Sundays excepted
exprés	slow night train
facturación	check-in
ferrobús	local short-distance train
fumadores	smokers
hacer transbordo en ...	change at ...
hora local	local time
horario	timetable
laborables	weekdays
libre	vacant
llegadas	arrivals
multa por uso indebido	penalty for misuse
nacional	domestic
niños	children
no fumadores	non-smokers
no para en ...	does not stop in ...
ocupado	engaged
pague el importe exacto	no change given
parada	stop
prensa	newspaper kiosk
prohibida la entrada	no entry
prohibido asomarse a la ventana	do not lean out of the window
prohibido el paso	no entry
prohibido fumar	no smoking
prohibido hablar con el conductor	do not speak to the driver
puerto	harbour
puerta de embarque	gate
puesto de periódicos	newspaper kiosk
rápido	slow train stopping at all stations
recogida de equipajes	baggage claim

→

RENFE	Spanish national railways
reserva de asientos	seat reservation
retraso	delay
ruta	route
sala de espera	waiting room
salida	departure; exit
salida de emergencia	emergency exit
salidas	departures
sólo laborables	weekdays only
suplemento	supplement
taco	book of underground tickets
TAF	slow diesel train
talgo	fast diesel train
taquilla	ticket office
TER	fast diesel train
terminal	terminus
trenes de cercanías	local trains
utilice solo moneda fraccionaria	small change only
vagón	carriage
viaje	journey
vuelo	flight
vuelo directo	direct flight
vuelo regular	scheduled flight

THINGS YOU'LL HEAR

¿Tiene equipaje?
Have you any luggage?

¿Fumadores o no fumadores?
Smoking or non-smoking?

¿Asiento de ventanilla o de pasillo?
Window seat or aisle seat?

→

Su billete, por favor
Can I see your ticket, please?

Los pasajeros del vuelo tres dos cuatro, con destino a Londres, están en estos momentos embarcando en el avión
Passengers for flight 324 for London are requested to board

Diríjanse a la puerta (número) cuatro
Please go now to gate (number) four

Completo
It's full

Los billetes, por favor
Tickets please

Suban al tren
Board the train

El tren con destino a Granada va a efectuar su salida del andén número seis dentro de diez minutos
The train for Granada will leave from platform six in ten minutes

El tren procedente de Madrid va a efectuar su llegada al andén número uno dentro de cinco minutos
The train from Madrid will arrive at platform one in five minutes

El tren con destino a Sevilla lleva quince minutos de retraso
The train for Seville is running 15 minutes late

Saquen sus billetes, por favor
Have your tickets ready, please

Su pasaporte, por favor
Your passport, please

Abra sus maletas, por favor
Open your suitcases, please

RESTAURANTS

You can eat in a variety of places:

Restaurante: These have an official rating (1-5 forks), but this depends more on the variety of dishes served than on the quality!

Cafetería: Not to be confused with the English term! It is a combined bar, café and restaurant. Service is provided at the counter or, for a little extra, at a table. There is usually a good variety of set menus at reasonable prices (look for **platos combinados**).

Fonda: Offers cheap, simple food which is usually good and representative of regional dishes.

Hostería or **Hostal**: A restaurant that usually specializes in regional dishes.

Parador: Belonging to the previously state-run hotels, they offer a first rate service in select surroundings.

Café or **Bar**: Both are general cafés selling all kinds of food and drink (again, they are not to be confused with English establishments of the same name). Well worth trying if you just want a quick snack. In some places they serve free **tapas** ('tasters') with alcoholic drinks. Full meals are often available.

Merendero: Open-air **café** on the coast or in the country. Usually cheap and good value.

Breakfast in Spain is at 7 am, lunch is at 2 pm and dinner (the main evening meal) at 10 pm.

USEFUL WORDS AND PHRASES

beer	una cerveza	*thairveh-tha*
bill	la cuenta	*kwenta*
bottle	la botella	*boh-tay-ya*

bread	el pan	*pan*
butter	la mantequilla	*manteh-kee-ya*
café	una cafetería	*kaffeh-teh-ree-a*
cake	un pastel	*pastell*
carafe	una jarra	*Harra*
chef	el cocinero	*kothee-neh-roh*
children's portion	una ración especial para niños	*rath-yon espethyal parra neen-yoss*
coffee	el café	*kaffeh*
cup	la taza	*tah-tha*
dessert	el postre	*postreh*
fork	el tenedor	*teneh-dor*
glass	el vaso	*vah-soh*
half-litre	medio litro	*meh-dyoh leetroh*
knife	el cuchillo	*kootchee-yoh*
litre	litro	*leetroh*
main course	el segundo plato	*segoondoh plah-toh*
menu	la carta	*karta*
milk	la leche	*letcheh*
pepper	la pimienta	*peemyenta*
plate	el plato	*plah-toh*
receipt	un recibo	*retheeboh*
restaurant	un restaurante	*restowranteh*
salt	la sal	*sal*
sandwich *(Spanish)*	un sandwich un bocadillo	*sand-weetch boh-kadee-yoh*
serviette	la servilleta	*sairvee-yeh-ta*
soup	la sopa	*soh-pa*
spoon	la cuchara	*kootchah-ra*
starter	el primer plato	*primair plah-toh*
sugar	el azúcar	*athookar*
table	una mesa	*meh-sa*
tea	el té	*teh*
teaspoon	la cucharilla	*kootcha-ree-ya*
tip	una propina	*propeena*
waiter	el camarero	*kamma-reh-roh*
waitress	la camarera	*kamma-reh-ra*

water	el agua	_ahg-wa_
wine	el vino	_veenoh_
wine list	la carta de vinos	_karta deh veenoss_

A table for one please
Una mesa para una persona, por favor
oona meh-sa parra oona pairsoh-na por fa-vor

A table for two/three please
Una mesa para dos/tres personas, por favor
oona meh-sa parra doss/tress pairsoh-nass por fa-vor

Can we see the menu/wine list?
¿Nos trae la carta/la carta de vinos?
noss trah-eh la karta/la karta deh veenoss

What would you recommend?
¿Qué recomendaría usted?
keh rekomenda-ree-a oosteh

I'd like ...
Quería ...
keh-ree-a

Just a cup of coffee, please
Un café nada más, por favor
oon kaffeh nah-da mass por fa-vor

I only want a snack
Sólo quiero una comida ligera
soh-loh kee-eh-roh oona kommeeda lee-Heh-ra

Is there a set menu?
¿Hay plato del día?
I plah-toh dell dee-a

A litre carafe of house red, please
Una jarra de litro de tinto de la casa, por favor
oona Harra deh leetroh deh teentoh deh la kah-sa por fa-vor

Do you have any vegetarian dishes?
¿Tiene algún plato vegetariano?
tyeh-neh algoon plah-toh veh-Hetaryah-noh

Could we have some water?
¿Nos trae agua, por favor?
noss trah-eh ahg-wa por fa-vor

Two more beers please
Dos cervezas más, por favor
doss thair-veh-thass mass por fa-vor

Do you do children's portions?
¿Tiene raciones especiales para niños?
tyeh-neh rathyoh-ness espethyah-less parra neen-yoss

Waiter/waitress!
¡Camarero!/¡Señorita!
kamma-reh-roh/sen-yorreeta

I didn't order this
No he pedido esto
noh eh pedeedoh estoh

You've forgotten to bring my dessert
Se ha olvidado de traerme el postre
seh a olveedah-doh deh trah-airmeh el postreh

May we have some more ...?
¿Nos trae más ...?
noss trah-eh mass

Can I have another knife/fork?
¿Me trae otro cuchillo/tenedor?
meh trah-eh otroh kootchee-yoh/teneh-dor

Can we have the bill, please?
¿Nos trae la cuenta, por favor?
noss trah-eh la kwenta por fa-vor

Could I have a receipt, please?
¿Me puede dar un recibo, por favor?
meh pweh-deh dar oon retheeboh por fa-vor

Can we pay separately?
Queríamos pagar por separado
keh-ree-amoss pagar por separah-doh

The meal was very good, thank you
La comida ha sido muy buena, gracias
la kommeeda a seedoh mwee bweh-na grath-yass

My compliments to the chef!
¡Felicite al cocinero de mi parte!
felee-theeteh al kothee-neh-roh deh mee parteh

YOU MAY HEAR

¡Que (le/les) aproveche!
Enjoy your meal!

¿Qué quiere para beber/tomar?
What would you like to drink?

¿Le ha gustado la comida?
Did you enjoy your meal?

MENU GUIDE

aceitunas	olives
acelgas	spinach beet
achicoria	chicory
aguacate	avocado
ahumados	smoked fish
ajo	garlic
albaricoques	apricots
albóndigas	meat balls
alcachofas	artichokes
alcachofas con jamón	artichokes with ham
alcachofas salteadas	sautéed artichokes
alcachofas vinagreta	artichokes vinaigrette
alcaparras	capers
almejas	clams
almejas a la marinera	clams stewed in wine and parsley
almejas naturales	live clams
almendras	almonds
alubias con ...	beans with ...
ancas de rana	frogs' legs
anchoas	anchovies
anguila	eel
angulas	baby eels
anís	aniseed-flavoured alcoholic drink
arenque	herring
arroz a la cubana	rice with fried eggs and banana fritters
arroz a la valenciana	rice with seafood
arroz con leche	rice pudding
asados	roast meats
atún	tuna
avellanas	hazelnuts
azúcar	sugar
bacalao a la vizcaína	cod served with ham, peppers and chillis
bacalao al pil pil	cod served with chillis and garlic
batido de chocolate	chocolate milkshake
batido de fresa	strawberry milkshake
batido de frutas	fruit milkshake

batido de vainilla	vanilla milkshake
bebidas	drinks
berenjenas	aubergines
berza	cabbage
besugo al horno	baked sea bream
bistec de ternera	veal steak
bizcochos	sponge fingers
bonito al horno	baked tuna fish
bonito con tomate	tuna with tomato
boquerones fritos	fried anchovies
brazo de gitano	swiss roll
brevas	figs
broqueta de riñones	kidney kebabs
buñuelos	light fried pastries
butifarra	Catalan sausage (made with a large proportion of bacon)
cabrito asado	roast kid
cachelada	pork stew with eggs, tomato and onion
café	coffee
café con leche	white coffee
calabacines	courgettes, marrow
calabaza	pumpkin
calamares a la romana	squid rings in batter
calamares en su tinta	squid cooked in their ink
calamares fritos	fried squid
caldeirada	fish soup
caldereta gallega	vegetable stew
caldo de ...	... soup
caldo de gallina	chicken soup
caldo de pescado	clear fish soup
caldo gallego	vegetable soup
caldo guanche	soup made with potatoes, onions, tomatoes and courgettes
callos a la madrileña	tripe cooked with chillis
camarones	baby prawns
canelones	canneloni
cangrejos de río	river crabs
caracoles	snails
caramelos	sweets
carnes	meats
carro de queso	cheese board

castañas	chestnuts
cebolla	onion
cebolletas	spring onions
centollo	spider crab
cerezas	cherries
cerveza	beer
cesta de frutas	a selection of fresh fruit
champiñón a la crema	mushrooms in cream sauce
champiñón al ajillo	mushrooms with garlic
champiñón a la plancha	grilled mushrooms
champiñón salteado	sautéed mushrooms
chanquetes	fish (similar to whitebait)
chateaubrian	Chateaubriand steak *(thick steak)*
chipirones	squid
chipirones en su tinta	squid cooked in their ink
chipirones rellenos	stuffed squid
chirimoyas	custard apples
chocos	squid
chuleta de buey	beef chop
chuleta de cerdo	pork chop
chuleta de cerdo empanada	breaded pork chop
chuleta de cordero	lamb chop
chuleta de ternera	veal chop
chuleta de ternera empanada	breaded veal chop
chuletas de cordero empanadas	breaded lamb chops
chuletas de lomo ahumado	smoked pork chops
chuletitas de cordero	small lamb chops
chuletón	large chop
chuletón de buey	large beef chop
churros	deep-fried pastry strips
cigalas	crayfish
cigalas cocidas	boiled crayfish
ciruelas	plums, greengages
ciruelas pasas	prunes
cochinillo asado	roast sucking pig
cocido	stew made with meat, chickpeas and vegetables
cocktail de bogavante	lobster cocktail
cocochas (de merluza)	hake stew
cóctel de gambas	prawn cocktail
cóctel de langostinos	king prawn cocktail
cóctel de mariscos	seafood cocktail

codornices	quail
codornices asadas	roast quail
codornices con uvas	quail stewed with grapes
codornices escabechadas	marinated quail
codornices estofadas	braised quail
col	cabbage
coles de Bruselas	Brussels sprouts
coles de Bruselas salteadas	sautéed Brussels sprouts
coliflor	cauliflower
coliflor con bechamel	cauliflower cheese
coñac	brandy
conejo asado	roast rabbit
conejo encebollado	rabbit served with onions
conejo estofado	braised rabbit
congrio	conger eel
consomé al jerez	consommé with sherry
consomé con yema	consommé with egg yolk
consomé de ave	chicken consommé
consomé de pollo	chicken consommé
contra de ternera con guisantes	veal stew with peas
contrafilete de ternera	veal fillet
copa ...	... cup
copa de helado	ice cream, assorted flavours
cordero asado	roast lamb
cordero chilindrón	lamb stew with onion, tomato, peppers and eggs
costillas de cerdo	pork ribs
crema catalana	crème brûlée
cremada	dessert made with egg, sugar and milk
crema de cangrejos	cream of crab soup
crema de espárragos	cream of asparagus soup
crema de legumbres	cream of vegetable soup
crepe imperiale	crêpe suzette
criadillas de tierra	truffles, usually served with meat dishes
crocante	ice cream with chopped nuts
croquetas	croquettes
croquetas de jamón	ham croquettes
croquetas de pescado	fish croquettes
cuajada	curds
dátiles	dates
embutidos	sausages

embutidos de la tierra	local sausages
embutidos variados	assorted sausages
empanada gallega	fish pie
empanada santiaguesa	fish pie
empanadillas de bonito	small tuna pies
empanadillas de carne	small meat pies
empanadillas de chorizo	Spanish sausage pies
endivias	endive
ensaimada mallorquina	large, spiral-shaped bun
ensalada de arenque	fish salad
ensalada de atún	tuna salad
ensalada de frutas	fruit salad
ensalada de gambas	prawn salad
ensalada de lechuga	lettuce salad
ensalada de pollo	chicken salad
ensalada de tomate	tomato salad
ensalada ilustrada	mixed salad
ensalada mixta	mixed salad
ensalada simple	green salad
ensaladilla	Spanish salad
ensaladilla rusa	Russian salad (potatoes, carrots, peas and other vegetables in mayonnaise)
entrecot a la parrilla	grilled entrecôte
entrecot de ternera	veal entrecôte
entremeses de la casa	hors d'oeuvres, starters
entremeses variados	hors d'oeuvres, starters
escalope a la milanesa	breaded veal with cheese
escalope a la parrilla	grilled veal
escalope a la plancha	grilled veal
escalope de lomo de cerdo	escalope of fillet of pork
escalope de ternera	veal escalope
escalope empanado	breaded escalope
escalopines al vino de Marsala	veal escalopes cooked in wine
escalopines de ternera	veal escalopes
escarola	crinkly lettuce
espadín a la toledana	kebab
espaguetis italiana	spaghetti
espárragos	asparagus
espárragos con mayonesa	asparagus with mayonnaise
espárragos trigueros	green asparagus
espinacas	spinach
espinacas a la crema	creamed spinach

espinazo de cerdo con patatas	stew of pork ribs with potatoes
estofado de ...	... stew
estofado de liebre	hare stew
estofados	stews
estragón	tarragon
fabada (asturiana)	bean stew with sausage
faisán con castañas	pheasant with chestnuts
faisán estofado	stewed pheasant
faisán trufado	pheasant with truffles
fiambres	cold meats
fideos	thin pasta, noodles
filete a la parrilla	grilled beef
filete de cerdo	pork steak
filete de ternera	veal steak
flan	crème caramel
flan al ron	crème caramel with rum
flan de caramelo	crème caramel
fresas con nata	strawberries and cream
fruta	fruit
frutas en almíbar	fruit in syrup
fruta variada	assorted fresh fruit
gallina en pepitoria	chicken stewed with peppers
gambas al ajillo	garlic prawns
gambas a la americana	prawns
gambas a la plancha	grilled prawns
gambas cocidas	boiled prawns
gambas con mayonesa	prawns with mayonnaise
gambas en gabardina	prawns in butter
gambas rebozadas	prawns in batter
garbanzos	chickpeas
garbanzos a la catalana	chickpeas with sausage, boiled eggs and pine nuts
gazpacho andaluz	cold tomato soup from Andalusia
gelatina de ...	... jelly
gratén de ...	... au gratin (baked in a cream and cheese sauce)
grelo	turnip
guisantes con jamón	peas with ham
guisantes salteados	sautéed peas
habas	broad beans
habas con jamón	broad beans with ham
habas fritas	fried young broad beans

habichuelas	beans
helado de caramelo	caramel ice cream
helado de chocolate	chocolate ice cream
helado de fresa	strawberry ice cream
helado de man•ecado	vanilla ice cream
helado de nata	dairy ice cream
helado de turrón	nut ice cream
helado de vainilla	vanilla ice cream
hígado	liver
hígado con cebolla	liver cooked with onion
hígado de ternera estofado	braised calf's liver
hígado estofado	braised liver
higos con miel y nueces	figs with honey and nuts
higos secos	dried figs
horchata (de chufas)	cold almond-flavoured milk drink
huevo hilado	egg yolk garnish
huevos	eggs
huevos a la flamenca	fried eggs with ham, tomato and vegetables
huevos cocidos	hard-boiled eggs
huevos con jamón	eggs with ham
huevos duros	hard-boiled eggs
huevos duros con mayonesa	boiled eggs with mayonnaise
huevos con panceta	eggs and bacon
huevos con patatas fritas	fried eggs and chips
huevos con picadillo	eggs with minced sausage
huevos con salchichas	eggs and sausages
huevos escalfados	poached eggs
huevos fritos	fried eggs
huevos fritos con chorizo	fried eggs with Spanish sausage
huevos fritos con jamón	fried eggs with ham
huevos pasados por agua	soft-boiled eggs
huevos rellenos	stuffed eggs
huevos revueltos con tomate	scrambled eggs with tomato
jamón con huevo hilado	ham with egg yolk garnish
jamón de Jabugo	Spanish ham
jamón de Trevélez	Spanish ham
jamón serrano	cured ham
jarra de vino	wine jug
jerez amontillado	pale dry sherry
jerez fino	pale light sherry
jerez oloroso	sweet sherry

jeta	pigs' cheeks
judías verdes	green beans
judías verdes a la española	bean stew
judías verdes al natural	plain green beans
judías verdes con jamón	green beans with ham
jugo de albaricoque	apricot juice
jugo de lima	lime juice
jugo de limón	lemon juice
jugo de melocotón	peach juice
jugo de naranja	orange juice
jugo de piña	pineapple juice
jugo de tomate	tomato juice
Jumilla	light red and white 'mistela' wines
langosta a la americana	lobster with brandy and garlic
langosta a la catalana	lobster with mushrooms and ham in a white sauce
langosta fría con mayonesa	cold lobster with mayonnaise
langosta gratinada	lobster au gratin
langostinos a la plancha	grilled king prawns
langostinos con mayonesa	king prawns with mayonnaise
langostinos dos salsas	king prawns cooked in two sauces
laurel	bay leaves
leche frita	pudding made from milk and eggs
leche merengada	cold milk with meringues
lechuga	lettuce
lengua de buey	ox tongue
lengua de cordero estofada	stewed lambs' tongue
lenguado a la parrilla	grilled sole
lenguado a la plancha	grilled sole
lenguado a la romana	sole in batter
lenguado frito	fried sole
lenguado grillado	grilled sole
lenguado meuniere	sole meunière (sole dipped in flour, fried and served with butter, lemon juice and parsley)
lentejas	lentils
lentejas aliñadas	lentils in vinaigrette dressing
licores	spirits, liqueurs
liebre estofada	stewed hare
lombarda rellena	stuffed red cabbage
lombarda salteada	sautéed red cabbage
lomo curado	pork-loin sausage

lonchas de jamón	sliced, cured ham
longaniza	cooked Spanish sausage
lubina a la marinera	sea bass in a parsley sauce
lubina al horno	baked sea bass
macarrones	macaroni
macarrones gratinados	macaroni cheese
macedonia de fruta	fruit salad
Málaga	sweet wine
mandarinas	tangerines
manises	peanuts
manitas de cordero	lamb shank
manos de cerdo	pigs' trotters
manos de cerdo a la parrilla	grilled pigs' trotters
mantecadas	small sponge cakes
mantequilla	butter
manzanas	apples
manzanas asadas	baked apples
manzanilla	dry sherry-type wine
mariscada	cold mixed shellfish
mariscos del día	fresh shellfish
mariscos del tiempo	seasonal shellfish
mazápan	marzipan
medallones de anguila	eel steaks
medallones de merluza	hake steaks
media de agua	half-bottle of mineral water
mejillones	mussels
mejillones a la marinera	mussels in a wine sauce
melocotón	peach
melocotones en almíbar	peaches in syrup
melón	melon
melón con jamón	melon with ham
membrillo	quince jelly
menestra de legumbres	vegetable stew
menú de la casa	fixed price menu
menú del día	set menu
merluza a la cazuela	stewed hake
merluza a la parrilla	grilled hake
merluza a la plancha	grilled hake
merluza a la riojana	hake with chillies
merluza a la romana	hake steaks in batter
merluza a la vasca	hake in a garlic sauce
merluza al ajo arriero	hake with garlic and chillies

merluza en salsa	hake in sauce
merluza en salsa verde	hake in a parsley and wine sauce
merluza fría	cold hake
merluza frita	fried hake
mermelada	jam
mermelada de albaricoque	apricot jam
mermelada de ciruelas	prune jam
mermelada de frambuesas	raspberry jam
mermelada de fresas	strawberry jam
mermelada de limón	lemon marmalade
mermelade de melocotón	peach jam
mermelada de naranja	orange marmalade
mero	grouper *(type of fish)*
mero a la parrilla	grilled grouper
mero en salsa verde	grouper in garlic and parsley sauce
mollejas de ternera fritas	fried sweetbreads
morcilla	black pudding
morcilla de carnero	black pudding made from mutton
morros de cerdo	pigs' cheeks
morros de vaca	cows' cheeks
mortadela	salami-type sausage
morteruelo	kind of mince pie
mousse de chocolate	chocolate mousse
mousse de limón	lemon mousse
nabo	turnip
naranjas	oranges
natillas	cold custard
natillas de chocolate	cold custard with chocolate
níscalos	wild mushrooms
nísperos	medlars *(fruit similar to crab apple)*
nueces	walnuts
orejas de cerdo	pigs' ears
otros mariscos según precios en plaza	other shellfish, depending on current prices
paella	fried rice with various seafood and chicken
paella castellana	meat *paella*
paella de marisco	shellfish *paella*
paella de pollo	chicken *paella*
paella valenciana	shellfish and chicken *paella*
paleta de cordero lechal	shoulder of lamb
pan	bread

pan de higos	dried fig cake with cinnamon
panache de verduras	vegetable stew
panceta	bacon
parrillada de caza	mixed grilled game
parrillada de mariscos	mixed grilled shellfish
pasas	raisins
pastel de ...	... cake
pastel de ternera	veal pie
pasteles	cakes
patatas a la pescadora	potatoes with fish
patatas asadas	baked potatoes
patatas bravas	potatoes in cayenne pepper sauce
patatas fritas	chips; crisps
patitos rellenos	stuffed duckling
pato a la naranja	duck à l'orange
pato asado	roast duck
pato estofado	stewed duck
pavipollo	large chicken
pavo asado	roast turkey
pavo relleno	stuffed turkey
pavo trufado	turkey stuffed with truffles
pecho de ternera	breast of veal
pechuga de pollo	breast of chicken
pepinillos	gherkins
pepinillos en vinagreta	gherkins in vinaigrette sauce
pepino	cucumber
peras	pears
percebes	edible barnacle *(shellfish)*
perdices a la campesina	partridges with vegetables
perdices a la manchega	partridges in red wine with garlic, herbs and pepper
perdices asadas	roast partridges
perdices con chocolate	partridges with chocolate sauce
perdices escabechadas	marinated partridges
perejil	parsley
pescaditos fritos	fried fish
pestiños	sugared pastries flavoured with aniseed
pez espada ahumado	smoked swordfish
picadillo de ternera	minced veal
pimienta	black pepper

pimientos a la riojana	baked red peppers fried in oil and garlic
pimientos fritos	fried peppers
pimientos morrones	strong peppers
pimientos rellenos	stuffed peppers
pimientos verdes	green peppers
piña al gratín	pineapple au gratin
piña fresca	fresh pineapple
pinchitos	snacks served in bars
pinchos	snacks served in bars
pinchos morunos	kebabs
piñones	pine nuts
pisto	fried mixed vegetables
pisto manchego	marrow with onion and tomato
plátanos	bananas
plátanos flameados	flambéed bananas
pollo a la parrilla	grilled chicken
pollo a la riojana	chicken with peppers and chillis
pollo al ajillo	fried chicken with garlic
pollo al champaña	chicken in champagne
pollo al vino blanco	chicken in white wine
pollo asado	roast chicken
pollo braseado	braised chicken
pollo con tomate	chicken with tomatoes
pollo con verduras	chicken and vegetables
pollo en cacerola	chicken casserole
pollo en pepitoria	chicken in wine with saffron, garlic and almonds
pollo salteado	sautéed chicken
pollos tomateros con zanhorias	young chicken with carrots
polvorones	sugar-based dessert eaten at Christmas
pomelo	grapefruit
potaje castellano	thick broth
potaje de garbanzos	chickpea stew
potaje de habichuelas	white bean stew
potaje de lentejas	lentil stew
puchero canario	casserole of meat, chickpeas and corn
pulpitos con cebolla	baby octopus with onions
pulpo	octopus
puré de patatas	mashed potatoes, potato purée
purrusalda	cod with leeks and potatoes

queso con membrillo	cheese with quince jelly
queso de Burgos	soft white cheese
queso de bola	Dutch cheese
queso de oveja	sheep's cheese
queso del país	local cheese
queso gallego	creamy cheese
queso manchego	hard, strong cheese
quisquillas	shrimps
rábanos	radish
ragout de ternera	veal ragoût
rape a la americana	monkfish with brandy and herbs
rape a la cazuela	stewed monkfish
rape a la plancha	grilled monkfish
raviolis	ravioli
raya	skate
redondo al horno	roast fillet of beef
remolacha	beetroot
repollo	cabbage
repostería de la casa	cakes baked on the premises
requesón	cream cheese, cottage cheese
revuelto de ajos tiernos	scrambled eggs with spring garlic
revuelto de angulas	scrambled eggs with baby eels
revuelto de gambas	scrambled eggs with prawns
revuelto de sesos	scrambled eggs with brains
revuelto de trigueros	scrambled eggs with asparagus
revuelto mixto	scrambled eggs with mixed vegetables
Ribeiro	type of white wine
riñones	kidneys
riñones al jerez	kidneys with sherry
Rioja	red or white wine – considered the finest wine in Spain
rodaballo	turbot
romero	rosemary
ron	rum
roscas	sweet pastries
sal	salt
salchichas	sausages
salchichas de Frankfurt	frankfurters
salchichón	white sausage with pepper
salmón a la parrilla	grilled salmon
salmón ahumado	smoked salmon
salmón frío	cold salmon

salmonetes	red mullet
salmonetes a la parrilla	grilled red mullet
salmonetes en papillote	red mullet cooked in foil
salmorejo	thick sauce made with bread, tomatoes, olive oil, vinegar, green pepper and garlic, usually served with hard-boiled eggs
salpicón de mariscos	shellfish with vinaigrette
salsa allioli or ali oli	mayonnaise with garlic
salsa bechamel	white sauce
salsa de tomate	tomato sauce
salsa holandesa	hollandaise sauce (hot sauce made with eggs and butter)
salsa mahonesa or mayonesa	mayonnaise
salsa tártara	tartare sauce
salsa vinagreta	vinaigrette sauce
sandía	water melon
sangría	*sangría* (mixture of red wine, lemonade, spirits and fruit)
sardinas a la brasa	barbecued sardines
sardinas a la parrilla	grilled sardines
sardinas fritas	fried sardines
seco	dry
semidulce	medium-sweet
sesos a la romana	fried brains in batter
sesos rebozados	brains in batter
setas a la plancha	grilled mushrooms
setas rellenas	stuffed mushrooms
sidra	cider
sobreasada	soft red sausage with cayenne pepper
solomillo con guisantes	fillet steak with peas
solomillo con patatas	fillet steak with chips
solomillo de ternera	fillet of veal
solomillo de vaca	fillet of beef
solomillo frio	cold roast beef
sopa	soup
sopa castellana	vegetable soup
sopa de ajo	garlic soup
sopa de almendras	almond-based pudding
sopa de cola de buey	oxtail soup
sopa de fideos	noodle soup
sopa de gallina	chicken soup

sopa del día	soup of the day
sopa de legumbres	vegetable soup
sopa de lentejas	lentil soup
sopa de marisco	fish and shellfish soup
sopa de pescado	fish soup
sopa de rabo de buey	oxtail soup
sopa de verduras	vegetable soup
sopa mallorquina	soup with tomato, meat and eggs
sopa sevillana	fish and mayonnaise soup
sorbete	sorbet
soufflé	soufflé
soufflé de fresones	strawberry soufflé
soufflé de naranja	orange soufflé
soufflé de queso	cheese soufflé
suplemento de verduras	extra vegetables
tallarines	noodles
tallarines a la italiana	tagliatelle
tarta de almendra	almond gâteau
tarta de chocolate	chocolate gâteau
tarta de fresas	strawberry tart or gâteau
tarta de la casa	gâteau baked on the premises
tarta de manzana	apple tart
tarta helada	ice-cream gâteau
tarta moca	mocha tart
tencas	tench
ternera asada	roast veal
tocinillos de cielo	crème caramel
tomates rellenos	stuffed tomatoes
tomillo	thyme
tordo	thrush
torrijas	sweet pastries
tortilla Alaska	baked Alaska
tortilla a la paisana	omelette with a variety of vegetables
tortilla a su gusto	omelette made to the customer's wishes
tortilla de bonito	tuna omelette
tortilla de champiñones	mushroom omelette
tortilla de chorizo	omelette containing spiced sausage
tortilla de escabeche	fish omelette
tortilla de espárragos	asparagus omelette
tortilla de gambas	prawn omelette
tortilla de jamón	ham omelette

tortilla de patatas	potato omelette
tortilla de sesos	brain omlette
tortilla de setas	mushroom omlette
tortilla española	Spanish omlette with potato, onion and garlic
tortilla sacromonte	vegetable, brains and sausage omelette
tortillas variadas	assorted omelettes
tournedó	tournedos *(fillet steak)*
trucha ahumada	smoked trout
trucha con jamón	trout with ham
trucha escabechada	marinated trout
truchas a la marinera	trout in wine sauce
truchas molinera	trout meunière (trout dipped in flour, fried and served with butter, lemon juice and parsley)
trufas	truffles
turrón	nougat
turrón de Alicante	hard nougat
turrón de Jijona	soft nougat
turrón de coco	coconut nougat
turrón de yema	nougat with egg yolk
uvas	grapes
Valdepeñas	type of fruity red wine
vieiras	scallops
vino·blanco	white wine
vino de mesa	table wine
vino rosado	rosé wine
vino tinto	red wine
zanahorias a la crema	carrots à la crème
zarzuela de mariscos	seafood stew
zarzuela de pescados y mariscos	fish and shellfish stew
zumo de ...	... juice
zumo de albaricoque	apricot juice
zumo de lima	lime juice
zumo de limón	lemon juice
zumo de melocotón	peach juice
zumo de naranja	orange juice
zumo de piña	pineapple juice
zumo de tomate	tomato juice

SHOPS AND SERVICES

This chapter covers all sorts of shopping needs and services, and to start with you'll find some general phrases which can be used in lots of different places – many of which are named in the list below. After the general phrases come some more specific requests and sentences to use when you've found what you need, be it food, clothing, repairs, film-developing, a haircut or haggling in the market. Don't forget to refer to the mini-dictionary for items you may be looking for.

The latest changes in the law allow shops to stay open as they wish, but most stick to the usual hours of 9 am to 1.30 pm and 4.30 pm to 7.30 pm. In summer, a longer lunch break means that shops stay open in the evenings from about 5 pm to 8.30 pm. Most shops close at 2 pm on Saturdays. Large department stores do not close for lunch and are open longer on Saturdays.

Toiletries and non-drug items can be bought from supermarkets and department stores or from a **perfumería**, where they'll probably cost a bit more. (See HEALTH page 113 for details about chemists.)

A hairdresser's is called a **peluquería**. A men's hairdresser is more often called a **barbería** – and is easily recognized by the traditional barber's pole or a similar device with red, white and blue stripes.

USEFUL WORDS AND PHRASES

antique shop	la tienda de antigüedades	*tyenda deh antee-gwehdah-dess*
audio equipment	aparatos de música	*aparah-toss deh moossika*
baker's	la panadería	*pannadeh-ree-a*
bookshop	la librería	*leebreh-ree-a*
boutique	la boutique	*booteek*
butcher's	la carnicería	*karnee-theh-ree-a*

buy	comprar	*komprar*
cake shop	la pastelería	*pasteh-leh-ree-a*
camera shop	la tienda de fotografía	*tyenda deh fotografee-a*
camping equipment	equipos de camping	*ekeeposs deh kampeen*
carrier bag	una bolsa	*bolsa*
cheap	barato	*barah-toh*
china	la porcelana	*porthelah-na*
confectioner's	la confitería	*konfeeteree-a*
cost	costar	*kostar*
craft shop	la tienda de artesanía	*tyenda deh artesanee-a*
department store	los grandes almacenes	*grandess almatheh-ness*
dry cleaner's	la tintorería	*teentoreree-a*
electrical goods store	la eléctrica	*elektreeka*
expensive	caro	*kah-roh*
fishmonger's	la pescadería	*peskadeh-ree-a*
florist's	la floristería	*floreess-teh-ree-a*
food store	la tienda de alimentación	*tyenda deh aleementath-yon*
gift shop	la tienda de regalos	*tyenda deh regah-loss*
greengrocer's	la frutería	*frooteree-a*
grocer's	la tienda de comestibles	*tyenda deh comestee-bless*
hairdresser's		
(men's)	la barbería	*barbeh-ree-a*
(women's)	la peluquería	*pelookeh-ree-a*
hardware shop	la ferretería	*ferreh-teh-ree-a*
hypermarket	el híper	*eepair*
indoor market	el mercado	*mairkah-doh*
jeweller's	la joyería	*Hoy-ehree-a*
ladies' wear	señoras	*sen-yorass*
launderette	la lavandería automática	*lavandereea owtoh-mateeka*
market	el mercadillo	*mairkadee-yoh*
menswear	caballeros	*kabayeh-ross*

newsagent's	el kiosko de periódicos	*kee-oskoh deh peh-ree-oddee-koss*
optician's	la óptica	*opteeka*
receipt	el recibo	*retheeboh*
record shop	la tienda de discos	*tyenda deh deeskoss*
sale	rebajas, liquidación	*rebah-Hass, leekee-dath-yon*
shoe repairer's	reparación del calzado	*reparath-yon del kalthah-doh*
shoe shop	la zapatería	*thapateh-ree-a*
shop	la tienda	*tyenda*
souvenir shop	la tienda de regalos	*tyenda deh regah-loss*
sports equipment	equipos de deporte	*eh-keeposs deh dehporteh*
sportswear	ropa de deporte	*roh-pa deh dehporteh*
stationer's	la papelería	*papeh-leh-ree-a*
supermarket	el supermercado	*sooper-mair-kah-doh*
tailor	la sastrería	*sastreh-ree-a*
till	la caja	*kah-Ha*
tobacconist's	el estanco	*estankoh*
toyshop	la juguetería	*Hoo-gheh-teh-ree-a*
travel agent's	la agencia de viajes	*aHenth-ya deh vyah-Hess*
wine merchant	la bodega de vinos	*boh-dehga deh veenoss*

Excuse me, where is/are ...? *(in a supermarket)*
Por favor, ¿dónde está/están ...?
por fa-vor dondeh esta/estan

Where is there a ... (shop)?
¿Dónde hay una (tienda de) ...?
dondeh I oona tyenda deh

Where is the ... department?
¿Dónde está la sección de ...?
dondeh esta la sekth-yon deh

Where is the main shopping area?
¿Dónde está la zona comercial?
dondeh esta la thona kommairth-yal

Is there a market here?
¿Hay algún mercadillo aquí?
I algoon mairkadee-yoh akee

I'd like …
Quería …
keh-ree-a

Do you have …?
¿Tienen …?
tyeh-nen

How much is this?
¿Cuánto es esto?
kwantoh ess estoh

Where do I pay?
¿Dónde se paga?
dondeh seh pah-ga

Do you take credit cards?
¿Puedo pagar con tarjeta de crédito?
pweh-doh pagar kon tar-Heh-ta deh kredeetoh

I think perhaps you've short-changed me
Me parece que me ha dado cambio de menos
meh pareh-theh keh meh a dadoh kamb-yoh deh menoss

Can I have a receipt?
¿Me da un recibo?
meh da oon retheeboh

Can I have a bag, please?
¿Me da una bolsa, por favor?
meh da oona bolsa por fa-vor

I'm just looking
Sólo estoy mirando
soh-loh estoy meerandoh

I'll come back later
Volveré luego
bolvereh lwehgoh

Do you have any more of these?
¿Tiene alguno más de éstos?
tyeh-neh algoonoh mass deh estoss

Have you anything cheaper?
¿Tiene usted algo más barato?
tyeh-neh oosteh algoh mass barah-toh

Have you anything larger/smaller?
¿Tiene usted algo más grande/pequeño?
tyeh-neh oosteh algoh mass grandeh/peh-kayn-yoh

Can I try it (them) on?
¿Puedo probármelo(s)?
pweh-doh probarmeh-loh(ss)

Does it come in other colours?
¿Lo hay en otros colores?
loh I en otross koloress

Could you gift-wrap it for me?
¿Podría envolvérmelo para regalo?
podree-a embol-vairmeh-loh parra regah-loh

I'd like to exchange this, it's faulty
Quiero que me cambien esto porque tiene un defecto
kyeh-roh keh meh kambyen estoh por-keh tyeh-neh oon defektoh

I'm afraid I don't have the receipt
Me temo que no tengo el ticket de compra
meh temoh keh noh teng-goh el teekeh deh kompra

Can I have a refund?
¿Pueden devolverme el dinero?
pweh-den deh-volvair-meh el deeneh-roh

My camera isn't working
Mi máquina (de fotos) no funciona
mee makeena deh fotos noh foonth-yoh-na

I want a 36-exposure colour film. 100 ISO
Quiero un carrete en color de treinta y seis fotos. De cien ISO
*kyeh-roh oon karreh-teh en kolor deh trayntI sayss fotos deh thyen
ee esseh oh*

I'd like this film processed
Quería revelar este carrete
kehree-a revelar esteh karreh-teh

Matt prints
Copias en papel mate
koh-pyass en pappell mateh

Glossy prints
Copias con brillo
koh-pyass kon bree-yoh

One-hour service, please
Servicio de una hora, por favor
sairveeth-yoh deh oona ora por fa-vor

Where can I get this mended?
¿Dónde me pueden arreglar esto?
dondeh meh pweh-den arreh-glar estoh

Can you mend this?
¿Puede arreglarme esto?
pweh-deh arrehglarmeh estoh

I'd like this skirt/these trousers dry-cleaned
Quiero que me limpien esta falda/estos pantalones
kyeh-roh keh meh leempyen esta falda/estoss pantaloh-ness

When will it (they) be ready?
¿Cuándo estará(n) listo(s)?
kwandoh estara(n) leestoh(ss)

I'd like some change for the washing machine/tumble dryer
¿Me puede cambiar dinero para la lavadora/secadora?
meh pweh-deh kambyar deeneh-roh parra la lavadora/sekadora

Can you help me work the machine, please?
¿Puede enseñarme a manejar la máquina, por favor?
pweh-deh ensen-yarmeh a maneh-Har la makeena por fa-vor

I'd like to make an appointment
Quería pedir hora
keh-ree-a pedeer ora

I want a cut and blow-dry
Quería un corte y moldeado con secador de mano
keh-ree-a oon korteh ee moldeh-ah-doh kon sekador deh mah-noh

With conditioner/No conditioner, thanks
Con acondicionador/Sin acondicionador, por favor
kon akondeeth-yonador/seen akondeeth-yonador por fa-vor

Just a trim, please
Recórtemelo un poco solamente, por favor
rekorteh-meh-loh oon pokoh sola-menteh por fa-vor

A bit more off here, please
Córtemelo un poco más por aquí, por favor
korteh-meh-loh oon pokoh mass por akee por fa-vor

Not too much off!
¡No me corte demasiado!
noh meh korteh demass-yah-doh

When does the market open?
¿Cuándo se abre el mercadillo?
kwandoh seh ah-breh el mairkadee-yoh

What's the price per kilo?
¿Cuánto vale el kilo?
kwantoh valeh el keeloh

Could you write that down?
¿Puede escribírmelo?
pweh-deh eskreebeermeh-loh

That's too much! I'll pay ...
¡Eso es demasiado! Le doy ...
esso ess deh-mass-yah-doh! leh doy

I've seen that on another stall for ... pesetas
Lo he visto en otro puesto a ... pesetas
loh eh veestoh en otroh pwestoh a ... peh-seh-tass

That's fine. I'll take it
Está bien. Me lo llevo
esta byen. meh loh yeh-voh

I'll have a piece of that cheese
Quiero un trozo de ese queso
kyeh-roh oon troh-thoh deh esseh keh-soh

About 250/500 grams
Como doscientos cincuenta/quinientos gramos
koh-moh dossthyentoss theen-kwenta/keenyentoss grah-moss

A kilo/half a kilo of apples, please
Un kilo/medio kilo de manzanas, por favor
oon keeloh/meh-dyoh keeloh deh manthah-nass por fa-vor

A quarter of a kilo of ham, please
Un cuarto de kilo de jamón, por favor
oon kwartoh deh keeloh deh Hamon por fa-vor

May I taste it?
¿Puedo probarlo?
pweh-doh probarloh

No, I don't like it
No, no me gusta
noh noh meh goosta

That's very nice. I'll take some
Está muy bueno. Me llevaré un poco
esta mwee bweh-noh. meh yehvareh oon poh-koh

It isn't what I wanted
No es lo que yo quería
noh ess loh keh yoh keh-ree-a

THINGS YOU'LL SEE

abierto	open
agencia de viajes	travel agency
alimentación	groceries
alquiler	rental
autoservicio	self-service
barato	cheap
barbería	barber
bricolage	DIY supplies
caballeros	menswear
caja	till, cash desk
calidad	quality
calzados	shoe shop
carnicería	butcher's
cerrado	closed
cerrado por vacaciones	closed for holidays
cerramos los ...	closed on ...
droguería	household cleaning materials
estanco	tobacconist's
ferretería	hardware shop
flores	flowers

→

ganga	bargain
grandes almacenes	department store
helados	ice-cream shop
juguetes	toys
lavado	shampoo
librería	bookshop
liquidación total	stock clearance
moda	fashion
moldeado con secador de mano	blow-dry
no se admiten devoluciones	no refunds given
no tocar	do not touch
objetos de escritorio	office supplies
oferta	special offer
panadería	bakery
papelería	stationer's
pastelería	cake shop
peletería	furrier
peluquería de caballeros	men's hairdresser
peluquería de señoras	ladies' salon
planta sótano	lower floor
planta superior	upper floor
por favor, use una cesta/un carrito	please take a basket/trolley
precio	price
rea	sale
rebajado	reduced
rebajas	sales
rebajas de verano	summer sale
saldos	sales
salón de peluquería	hairdressing salon
sección	department
señoras	ladies' department
verduras	vegetables

THINGS YOU'LL HEAR

¿Le están atendiendo?
Are you being served?

¿Qué desea?
Can I help you?

¿No tiene más que eso?
Haven't you anything smaller? *(money)*

Lo siento, se nos han terminado
I'm sorry, we're out of stock

Esto es todo lo que tenemos
This is all we have

No podemos devolver el importe
We cannot give cash refunds

¿Desea algo más?
Will there be anything else?

¿Cuánto quería?
How much would you like?

¿Le importa que sea un poco más?
Does it matter if it's a bit over?

Lo siento, no admitimos tarjetas de crédito
I'm afraid we don't take credit cards

¿Cómo quiere que se lo corte?
How would you like it cut?

SPORT

Thanks to Spain's excellent climate almost all outdoor sports are well catered for. The east and south coasts especially provide excellent opportunities for swimming, water-skiing, sailing, fishing (including underwater fishing) and sailboarding. The north coast also has good facilities and is becoming more and more popular, despite the cooler climate. A flag warning system operates on most Atlantic beaches: red for dangerous conditions, yellow for caution and green for all-clear. Hiring equipment poses no problem and everything from a parasol to a sailboard is covered at a reasonable charge. Golf, which has become very popular, offers play all the year round and courses exist in Madrid and nearly all the major beach resorts. Most golf courses offer coaching. Tennis courts can be found in most places and squash is gaining in popularity. Cycling is very popular and there are now more and more places where you can hire bicycles. In areas such as the Pyrenees and the Sierra Nevada there is ample scope for walking, mountaineering, and skiing in the winter.

USEFUL WORDS AND PHRASES

athletics	el atletismo	atleh-_teez_moh
badminton	el badminton	b_a_dmeen-ton
ball	la pelota	peh-_loh_-ta
bicycle	una bicicleta	beethee-_kleh_-ta
binding *(ski)*	una atadura	atad_oo_ra
bull-fighting	los toros	_toh_-ross
canoe	una piragua	peer_ah_-gwa
canoeing	el piragüismo	peerag-_weez_moh
cross-country skiing	el esquí de fondo	esk_ee_ deh _fon_doh
current	una corriente	korry_e_nteh
cycle path	el carril para bicicletas	karr_eel_ p_a_rra beetheekl_eh_-tass

cycling	el ciclismo	*theekleezmoh*
dive	tirarse de cabeza	*teerarseh deh kabeh-tha*
diving board	un trampolín	*trampoh-leen*
fishing	la pesca	*peska*
fishing rod	una caña de pescar	*kahn-ya deh peskar*
flippers	las aletas	*aleh-tass*
football	el balón	*ba-lon*
football match	un partido de fútbol	*partee-doh deh foot-bol*
game	un juego	*Hweh-goh*
goggles	las gafas de bucear	*gah-fass deh bootheh-ar*
golf	el golf	*golf*
play golf	jugar al golf	*Hoogar al golf*
golf club *(stick)*	el palo	*paloh*
golf course	un campo de golf	*kampoh deh golf*
gymnastics	la gimnasia	*Heemnass-ya*
hang-gliding	el ala delta	*ala delta*
harpoon	el fusil submarino	*foo-seel soobma-reenoh*
go hillwalking	andar por las montañas	*andar por las montan-yass*
hockey	el hockey	*Hokkay*
hunting	la caza	*katha*
mast	el mástil	*masteel*
mountaineering	el montañismo	*montan-yeezmoh*
nursery slope	la pista de principiantes	*peesta deh preentheepyantess*
oxygen bottles	las botellas de oxígeno	*botay-yass deh oksee-Hennoh*
parascending	el parapente	*parapenteh*
pedal boat	un hidropedal	*eedroh-peh-dal*
piste	la pista	*peesta*
Pyrenees	los Pirineos	*peereeneh-oss*
racket	una raqueta	*rakeh-ta*
ride	montar a caballo	*montar a kaba-yoh*
riding	la equitación	*ekeetath-yon*
riding hat	el casco de equitación	*kaskoh deh ekeetath-yon*
rock climbing	el alpinismo	*alpeeneezmoh*

saddle	la silla	*see-ya*
sail *(noun)*	la vela	*veh-la*
(verb)	navegar (a vela)	*navegar a veh-la*
sailboard	una tabla de windsurfing	*tah-bla deh weendsoorfeen*
sailing	vela	*veh-la*
go sailing	hacer vela	*athair veh-la*
skate	patinar	*pateenar*
skates	los patines	*patee-ness*
skating rink	la pista de patinaje	*peesta deh pateenah-Heh*
ski *(noun)*	un esquí	*eskee*
(verb)	esquiar	*eskyar*
ski boots	las botas de esquí	*botass deh eskee*
skiing	el esquí	*eskee*
ski lift	el telesquí	*tehlehskee*
skin diving	el submarinismo	*soobmaree-neezmoh*
ski pass	un abono	*aboh-noh*
ski sticks	los bastones	*bastoh-ness*
ski tow	el remonte	*remonteh*
ski trail	la pista de fondo	*peesta deh fondoh*
ski wax	la cera de esquís	*theh-ra deh eskees*
sledge	el trineo	*treeneh-oh*
snorkel	el respirador	*resspeera-dor*
sports centre	el polideportivo	*poleedeporteevoh*
stadium	el estadio	*estah-dyoh*
surfboard	la tabla de surfing	*tabla deh soorfeen*
swim	nadar	*nadar*
swimming pool	la piscina	*peessthee-na*
team	el equipo	*ekeepoh*
tennis	el tenis	*teh-neess*
tennis court	una pista de tenis	*peesta deh teh-neess*
tennis racket	una raqueta de tenis	*rakeh-ta deh teh-neess*
toboggan	el tobogán	*tobogan*
underwater fishing	la pesca submarina	*peska soobmaree-na*
volleyball	el voléibol	*vollay-bol*

water-skiing	el esquí acuático	*eskee akwatee-koh*
water-skis	los esquís acuáticos	*eskeess akwatee-koss*
wet suit	un traje isotérmico	*trah-Heh eessoh-tairmee-koh*
go windsurfing	hacer windsurfing	*athair weendsoorfeen*
yacht	un yate	*yah-teh*

How do I get to the beach?
¿Por dónde se va a la playa?
por dondeh seh va a la pla-ya

How deep is the water here?
¿Qué profundidad tiene el agua aquí?
keh profoondee-da tyeh-neh el ah-gwa akee

Is there an indoor/outdoor pool here?
¿Hay piscina cubierta/al aire libre aquí?
I peessthee-na koob-yairta/al I-reh leebreh akee

Is it safe to swim here?
¿Se puede nadar sin peligro aquí?
seh pweh-deh nadar seen pelee-groh akee

Can I fish here?
¿Puedo pescar aquí?
pweh-doh peskar akee

Do I need a licence?
¿Necesito un permiso?
nethessee-toh oon pair-meessoh

Is there a golf course near here?
¿Hay algún campo de golf por aquí cerca?
I algoon kampoh deh golf por akee thairka

Do I have to be a member?
¿Es necesario ser socio?
ess nethessaryoh sair soh-thyoh

I would like to hire a bicycle/some skis
Quería alquilar una bicicleta/unos esquís
keh-ree-a alkee-lar oona beethee-kleh-ta/oonoss eskeess

How much does it cost per hour/day?
¿Cuánto cuesta por hora/por día?
kwantoh kwesta por ora/por dee-a

I would like to take water-skiing lessons
Quería dar clases de esquí acuático
keh-ree-a dar klah-sess deh eskee akwatee-koh

Where can I hire ...?
¿Dónde puedo alquilar ...?
dondeh pweh-doh alkee-lar

There's something wrong with this binding
No sé qué pasa con esta atadura
noh seh keh pah-sa kon esta atadoora

How much is a weekly pass for the ski lift?
¿Cuánto valen los abonos semanales para el telesquí?
kwantoh balen loss aboh-noss semanah-less parra el tehlehskee

What are the snow conditions like today?
¿Cuál es el estado de la nieve hoy?
kwal ess el estadoh deh la nyeh-veh oy

I'd like to try cross-country skiing
Me gustaría probar el esquí de fondo
meh goostaree-a probar el eskee deh fondoh

I haven't played this before
Nunca había jugado a esto antes
noonka abee-a Hoogah-doh a estoh antess

Let's go skating/swimming
Vamos a patinar/nadar
bah-moss a pateenar/nadar

What's the score?
¿A cómo van?
a koh-moh van

Who won?
¿Quién ha ganado?
kyen a ganadoh

THINGS YOU'LL SEE

acceso playa	to the beach
alquiler de barcos	boat hire
alquiler de bicicletas	bike hire
alquiler de esquís	(water-)ski hire
alquiler de sombrillas	sunshade hire
alquiler de tablas	board hire
alquiler de tumbonas	deckchair hire
camino privado	private entrance
campo de golf	golf course
corriente peligrosa	dangerous current
palos de golf	golf clubs
peatones	pedestrians
peligro	danger
piscina	swimming pool
piscina cubierta	indoor swimming pool
pista de tenis	tennis court
prohibido bañarse	no swimming
prohibido el paso	no trespassing
prohibido encender fuego	no fires
prohibido pescar	no fishing
remonte	ski tow
socorrista	lifeguard
telecabina	cable car
telesilla	chair lift
telesquí	ski lift

POST OFFICES AND BANKS

Post Offices in Spain deal only with mail and telegrams, so don't look for a phone there; use a call box or find the exchange (**Telefónica**). Stamps can be bought in the post office but most Spaniards go to an **estanco** (a state tobacconist shop – look for the brown and yellow sign) where you can also buy postcards. Post boxes are yellow.

Banks are only open in the morning, usually from 9 am to 1.30 pm Monday to Friday, although this may vary depending on where you are. They are also open on Saturdays until 1 pm. There are usually only one or two cashiers and first of all you have to go to the foreign exchange counter, **cambio**, and then queue up for the cashier. However, more and more banks in large towns are changing over to the British system where all transactions take place at the same counter. Cash dispensers are widespread and, in addition to credit cards, some will even accept British bank cards – check with your bank for details.

The Spanish unit of currency is the **peseta**. Coins come in denominations of 1, 5, 10, 25, 50, 100, 200 and 500 **pesetas**. Notes are available in 200, 500, 1,000, 2,000, 5,000 and 10,000 denominations.

USEFUL WORDS AND PHRASES

airmail	correo aéreo	*korreh-oh ah-aireh-oh*
bank	el banco	*bankoh*
banknote	un billete de banco	*bee-yehteh deh bankoh*
cash	dinero	*deeneroh*
cash dispenser	el cajero automático	*kah-Heroh owtomateekoh*
change	cambiar	*kambyar*
cheque	un cheque	*cheh-keh*
cheque book	el talonario de cheques	*talonaryoh deh cheh-kehss*

collection	la recogida	*reh-koh-Heeda*
counter	el mostrador	*mostra-dor*
credit card	la tarjeta de crédito	*tar-Heh-ta deh kredeetoh*
customs form	el impreso para la aduana	*eempreh-soh parra la advah-na*
delivery	el reparto	*reh-partoh*
deposit *(noun)*	un ingreso	*eengreh-soh*
(verb)	ingresar	*eengreh-sar*
exchange rate	el tipo de cambio	*teepoh deh kambyoh*
fax *(noun)*	un fax	*fax*
(verb: document)	mandar por fax	*mandar por fax*
fax machine	una máquina de fax	*oona makeena deh fax*
form	un impreso	*eempreh-soh*
international money order	un giro internacional	*Heeroh eentairnath-yonal*
letter	una carta	*karta*
mail	el correo	*korreh-oh*
money order	un giro (postal)	*Hee-roh postal*
package/parcel	un paquete	*pakeh-teh*
post *(noun)*	el correo	*korreh-oh*
(verb)	echar al buzón	*etchar al boothon*
postage rates	las tarifas postales	*tarree-fass postah-less*
postal order	un giro postal	*Hee-roh postal*
post box	el buzón	*boothon*
postcard	una postal	*postal*
postcode	el distrito postal	*deestree-toh postal*
poste-restante	la lista de correos	*leesta deh korreh-oss*
postman	el cartero	*karteh-roh*
post office	(la oficina de) correos	*offee-theena deh korreh-oss*
pound sterling	la libra esterlina	*leebra esterleena*
registered letter	una carta certificada	*karta thair-teefee-kah-da*
stamp	un sello	*say-yoh*
surface mail	correo ordinario	*korreh-oh ordee-nar-yoh*

telegram	un telegrama	*telleh-grah-ma*
traveller's cheque	un cheque de viaje	*cheh-keh deh vyah-Heh*
withdraw	retirar	*reteerar*
withdrawal	una retirada	*reteerah-da*

How much is a letter/postcard to England?
¿Qué franqueo lleva una carta/una postal a Inglaterra?
keh fran-keh-oh yeh-va oona karta/oona postal a eenglaterra

I would like three 45 peseta stamps
Quería tres sellos de cuarenta y cinco pesetas
keh-ree-a tress say-yoss deh kwarentI theenkoh pehseh-tass

I want to register this letter
Quiero mandar esta carta certificada
kee-eh-roh mandar esta karta thair-teefee-kah-da

I want to send this parcel to Scotland
Quiero mandar este paquete a Escocia
kee-eh-roh mandar esteh pakeh-teh a eskoh-thya

How long does the post to America take?
¿Cuánto tarda el correo para Estados Unidos?
kwantoh tarda el korreh-oh parra estah-doss ooneedoss

Where can I post this?
¿Dónde puedo echar esto?
dondeh pweh-doh etchar estoh

Is there any mail for me?
¿Hay algún correo para mí?
I algoon korreh-oh parra mee

I'd like to send a telegram/send a fax
Quería poner un telegrama/mandar un fax
keh-ree-a ponnair oon telleh-grah-ma/mandar oon fax

This is to go airmail
Esto quiero que vaya por avión
estoh kee-eh-roh keh va-ya por av-yon

I'd like to change this into pesetas
Quiero cambiar esto en pesetas
kee-eh-roh kambyar estoh en pehseh-tass

Can I cash these traveller's cheques?
Quisiera hacer efectivos estos cheques de viaje
keesyera athair efekteevoss estoss cheh-kess deh vyah-Heh

What is the exchange rate for the pound?
¿A cuánto está la libra?
a kwantoh esta la leebra

Can I draw cash using this credit card?
¿Puedo sacar dinero con esta tarjeta (de crédito)?
pweh-doh sakar deeneroh kon esta tar-Heh-ta deh kredeetoh

I'd like it in 5,000 peseta notes
¿Me lo puede dar en billetes de cinco mil, por favor?
meh loh pweh-deh dar en bee-yeh-tess deh theenkoh meel por fa-vor

Could you give me smaller notes?
¿Podría darme billetes de menor valor?
podree-a darmeh bee-yeh-tess deh menor valor

THINGS YOU'LL SEE

banco	bank
buzón	post box
caja	cashier
cajero automático	cash dispenser
cambio (de divisas)	currency exchange
cartas	letters
certificados	registered mail

➡

correo aéreo	airmail
correo urgente	express
cuentas corrientes	current accounts
destinatario	addressee
dirección	address
distrito postal	postcode
España	Spain *(inland postage)*
extranjero	postage abroad
franqueo	postage
giros	money orders
horas de oficina	opening hours
horas de recogida	collection times
ingresos	deposits
lista de correos	poste-restante
localidad	place
mercado de divisas	exchange rates
paquetes	parcels
postal	postcard
rellenar	to fill in
remitente	sender
sello	stamp
tarifa	charge
venta de sellos	stamps

TELEPHONES

Telephone boxes in Spain are metallic-grey and have the words **URBANA** (for local calls), **INTERURBANA**, (for long-distance calls) and **INTERNACIONAL** (for international calls) written on a green panel at the top. To call the UK or USA from an **internacional** kiosk, dial 07 and wait for a high-pitched tone, then dial 44 (for UK) or 1 (for USA) followed by the area code and the number you want. Remember to omit the 0 which prefixes all UK area codes.

The tones you hear on Spanish phones when making a call within Spain differ slightly from ours:

Dialling tone:	same as in UK or USA
Ringing:	repeated long tone
Engaged:	rapid pips

For international calls first insert several 100 peseta coins in the slot and then use smaller coins of 50 ptas to prolong the call. For local calls use 25 ptas coins, and for long-distance use 50 and 100 ptas.

There are also payphones in bars and restaurants, many of which have phones with a counter which is set to zero when you begin a call. Alternatively you can look for the **central telefónica** or **teléfonos** (telephone exchange) which are located in the centre of most towns. Run by **CTNE** (look for the initials, standing for Spain's national telephone company), these are sometimes open 24 hours a day in major towns. You ask at the cash desk for the number you want, go to a booth and wait for the call to be put through, and pay when you have finished your call. Another sign to look out for is **locutorio telefónico** where you'll find telephone booths which operate the same system as the **central telefónica** and which are located near the beach in main resorts. There are also private **locutorios** in major towns which, although they can be dearer, could save you a long trek to the **central telefónica**.

Cardphones are not yet widespread in Spain although you may find them in some cities, for example, Barcelona and Madrid.

USEFUL WORDS AND PHRASES

call *(noun)*	una llamada	*yamah-da*
(verb)	llamar	*yamar*
cardphone	un teléfono de tarjeta	*teh-leffonoh deh tar-Heh-ta*
code	el prefijo	*preh-fee-Hoh*
crossed line	un cruce de líneas	*kroo-theh deh leeneh-ass*
dial	marcar	*markar*
dialling tone	la señal para marcar	*sen-yal parra markar*
emergency	una emergencia	*emmair-Henth-ya*
enquiries	información	*eenformath-yon*
extension	extensión	*ekstenth-yon*
international	internacional	*eentair-nath-yonal*
number	el número	*noomeh-roh*
operator	la operadora	*opeh-radora*
payphone	un teléfono público	*teh-leffonoh poobleekoh*
phone box	una cabina telefónica	*kabeena tehleh-fonnika*
phonecard	una tarjeta de teléfono	*tar-Heh-ta deh teh-leffonoh*
phone directory	la guía telefónica	*gee-a tehleh-fonnika*
push-button phone	un teléfono automático	*teh-leffonoh owtoh-matikoh*
receiver	el aparato	*aparah-toh*
reverse charge call	una llamada a cobro revertido	*yamah-da a kobroh reh-vair-teedoh*
telephone	un teléfono	*teh-leffonoh*
wrong number	el número equivocado	*noomeh-roh eh-keevoh-kah-doh*

Where is the nearest phone box?
¿Dónde está la cabina telefónica más cercana?
dondeh esta la kabeena tehleh-fonnika mass thair-kah-na

Is there a phone directory?
¿Hay una guía telefónica?
I oona gee-a tehleh-fonnika

I would like the directory for Malaga
Quería la guía telefónica de Málaga
keh-ree-a la gee-a tehleh-fonnika deh malaga

Can I call abroad from here?
¿Puedo llamar al extranjero desde aquí?
pweh-doh yamar al estran-Heh-roh dezdeh akee

How much is a call to England?
¿Cuánto cuesta una llamada a Inglaterra?
kwantoh kwesta oona yamah-da a eenglaterra

YOU MAY HEAR

¿A dónde quiere llamar?
Where do you want to call?

Vaya a la cabina cuatro
Now go to booth number 4

I would like to reverse the charges
Quiero que sea a cobro revertido
kyeh-roh keh seh-a a koh-broh reh-vair-teedoh

I would like a number in Barcelona
Quiero un número de Barcelona
kyeh-roh oon noomeh-roh deh bartheh-lohna

Could you give me an outside line?
¿Puede darme línea, por favor?
pweh-deh dar-meh leeneh-a por fa-vor

103

How do I get an outside line?
¿Cómo puedo obtener línea?
koh-moh pweh-doh obtenair leeneh-a

Hello, this is Anne speaking
Hola, soy Anne
oh-la soy 'Anne'

Is that Fernando?
¿Es (usted) Fernando?
ess oosteh fairnandoh

Hello *(when answering)*
Dígame
dee-gah-meh

Speaking
Al habla
al abla

I would like to speak to Maria
Quería hablar con María
keh-ree-a ablar kon maree-a

Extension 345 please
Extensión tres cuatro cinco, por favor
ekstenss-yon tress kwatroh theenkoh por fa-vor

Please tell him/her David called
Haga el favor de decirle que ha llamado David
ah-ga el fa-vor deh deh-theerleh keh a yamah-doh 'David'

Would you ask him/her to call me back please
Dígale que me llame cuando vuelva
dee-gah-leh keh meh yah-meh kwandoh vwelva

Do you know where he/she is?
¿Sabe usted dónde está?
sah-beh oosteh dondeh esta

My number is 234 33 52
Mi teléfono es el dos, treinta y cuatro, treinta y tres, cincuenta y
    dos
*mee teh-leffonoh ess el doss, trayntI kwatroh, trayntI tress, theen-
    kwentI doss*

When will he/she be back?
¿Cuándo volverá?
kwandoh volveh-ra

Could you leave him/her a message?
¿Podría dejarle un recado?
podree-a deh-Harleh oon reh-kah-doh

I'll ring back later
Volveré a llamar luego
volveh-reh a yamar lweh-goh

Sorry, I've got the wrong number
Lo siento, me he equivocado de número
loh syen-toh meh eh ekeevoh-kah-doh deh noomeh-roh

Sorry, you've got the wrong number
Lo siento, pero se ha equivocado de número
loh syen-toh peh-roh seh a ekeevoh-kah-doh deh noomeh-roh

THE ALPHABET

a	*ah*	**g**	*Heh*	**n**	*eneh*	**t**	*teh*
b	*beh*	**h**	*acheh*	**ñ**	*enyeh*	**u**	*oo*
c	*theh*	**i**	*ee*	**o**	*o*	**v**	*oobeh*
ch	*cheh*	**j**	*Hota*	**p**	*peh*	**w**	*oobeh dobleh*
d	*deh*	**k**	*ka*	**q**	*koo*	**x**	*ekiss*
e	*eh*	**l**	*eleh*	**r**	*ereh*	**y**	*ee gryehga*
f	*efeh*	**m**	*emeh*	**s**	*eseh*	**z**	*thehta*

105

THINGS YOU'LL SEE

cabina telefónica	telephone box
central telefónica	telephone exchange
CTNE	Spanish national telephone company
descolgar el aparato	lift receiver
EEUU	USA
guía telefónica	telephone directory
insertar monedas	insert coins
interurbana	long-distance
llamada	call
locutorio telefónico	telephone booths
marcar el número	dial the number
monedas	coins
no funciona	out of order
número	number
operadora	operator
páginas amarillas	yellow pages
paso (de contador)	unit
prefijo	code
Reino Unido	UK
reparaciones	faults service
servicio a través de operadora	dialling through the operator
servicio automático	direct dialling
tarifa	charges
tarjeta telefónica	phonecard
urbana	local

REPLIES YOU MAY BE GIVEN

¿Con quién quiere que le ponga?
Who would you like to speak to?

→

Se ha equivocado de número
You've got the wrong number

¿Quién es?
Who's speaking?

Al aparato/Al habla/Soy yo
Speaking

Diga/Dígame
Hello

¿Cuál es su teléfono?
What is your number?

Lo siento, no está
Sorry, he/she's not in

Puede dejar un recado
You can leave a message

Volverá dentro de ... minutos/horas
He/she'll be back in ... minutes/hours

Vuelva a llamar mañana, por favor
Please call again tomorrow

Le diré que le/la ha llamado usted
I'll tell him/her you called

**Las líneas con Sevilla se encuentran ocupadas en este
momento. Repita la llamada dentro de unos minutos**
All lines to Seville are busy at the moment. Please call again in a
few minutes time.

EMERGENCIES

Information on local health services can be obtained from tourist information offices but in an emergency dial **091** for the police and they will put you through to the ambulance service or fire brigade since there is no national central number for these emergency services.

In case of sudden illness or accident, go to the nearest **casa de socorro** (emergency first-aid centre) or to an **urgencias** (hospital casualty department). If on the road – look for **puestos de socorro** – which is also an emergency first-aid centre.

In the event of your car breaking down, try and get to the nearest **taller** (garage for repairs) or, if this is not possible, to the nearest service station, where they will be able to advise you on who to phone. If you are a member of the RAC or AA, there is a reciprocal agreement with the **RACE** (**Real Automóvil Club de España**) under which you should be covered.

USEFUL WORDS AND PHRASES

accident	un accidente	*akthee-denteh*
ambulance	una ambulancia	*amboolanth-ya*
assault	agredir	*agreh-deer*
breakdown	una avería	*aveh-ree-a*
break down	tener una avería	*tenair oona aveh-ree-a*
breakdown recovery	servicio de grúa	*sairveeth-yoh deh groo-a*
burglar	un ladrón	*ladron*
burglary	un robo	*roh-boh*
casualty department	urgencias	*oor-Henth-yass*
crash	un accidente	*akthee-denteh*
emergency	una emergencia	*emair-Henth-ya*
fire	un fuego	*fwehgoh*
(large, arson)	un incendio	*eenthend-yoh*
fire brigade	los bomberos	*bombeh-ross*

flood	una inundación	_eenoondath-yon_
injured	herido	_ereedoh_
pickpocket	un carterista	_kartereesta_
police	la policía	_poleethee-a_
police station	la comisaría	_kommeessaree-a_
theft	un robo	_rohboh_
thief	un ladrón	_ladron_
tow	remolcar	_remolkar_

Help!
¡Socorro!
sokorroh

Look out!
¡Cuidado!
kweedah-doh

Stop!
¡Pare!
pareh

This is an emergency!
¡Esto es una emergencia!
estoh ess oona emair-Henth-ya

Get an ambulance!
¡Llame una ambulancia!
yah-meh oona amboolanth-ya

Hurry up!
¡Dése prisa!
deh-seh preessa

Please send an ambulance to ...
Haga el favor de mandar una ambulancia a ...
ah-ga el fa-vor deh mandar oona amboolanth-ya a

Please come to ...
Haga el favor de venir a ...
ah-ga el fa-vor deh veneer a

My address is …
Mi dirección es …
mee deerekth-yon ess

We've had a break-in
Hemos tenido un robo en la casa
ehmoss teneedoh oon rohboh en la kasa

There's a fire at …
Hay un fuego en …
I oon fwehgoh en

Someone's been injured/knocked down
Hay una persona herida/atropellada
I oona pairsona ereeda/atropeh-yah-da

He's passed out
Ha perdido el conocimiento
a pairdeedoh el konotheemyentoh

My passport/car has been stolen
Me han robado el pasaporte/el coche
meh an robah-doh el passaporteh/el kotcheh

I've lost my traveller's cheques
He perdido mis cheques de viaje
eh pairdeedoh meess cheh-kess deh vyah-Heh

I want to report a stolen credit card
Quiero denunciar el robo de una tarjeta de crédito
kyeh-roh denoonthyar el rohboh deh oona tar-Heh-ta deh kredeetoh

It was stolen from my room
Lo robaron de mi habitación
lo robah-ron deh mee abeetath-yon

I lost it in/at …
Lo perdí en …
lo pairdee en

My luggage has gone missing
Mi equipaje se ha perdido
mee ekeep<u>ah</u>-Heh seh a paird<u>ee</u>doh

Has my luggage turned up yet?
¿Ha aparecido ya mi equipaje?
a apareh-th<u>ee</u>doh ya mee ekeep<u>ah</u>-Heh

I've had a crash
He tenido un accidente
eh ten<u>ee</u>doh oon akthee-d<u>e</u>nteh

My car's been broken into
Me han forzado el coche
meh an forth<u>ah</u>-doh el k<u>o</u>tcheh

The registration number is ...
El número de matrícula es el ...
el n<u>oo</u>meroh deh matr<u>ee</u>koola ess el

I've been mugged
Me han atacado
meh an atak<u>ah</u>-doh

My son's missing
Mi hijo se ha perdido
mee <u>ee</u>-Hoh seh a paird<u>ee</u>do

He has fair/brown hair
Tiene el pelo rubio/moreno
ty<u>eh</u>-neh el p<u>eh</u>-loh r<u>oo</u>b-yoh/mor<u>eh</u>-noh

He's ... years old
Tiene ... años
ty<u>eh</u>-neh ... <u>ah</u>n-yoss

I've locked myself out of my house/room/car
Me he dejado la llave dentro de la casa/habitación/del coche
meh eh deh-H<u>ah</u>-doh la y<u>ah</u>-veh d<u>e</u>ntroh deh la k<u>a</u>sa/abeetath-y<u>o</u>n/ del k<u>o</u>tcheh

He's drowning
Se está ahogando
seh est<u>a</u> ah-oh-g<u>a</u>ndoh

She can't swim
No sabe nadar
noh s<u>a</u>beh nad<u>a</u>r

THINGS YOU'LL SEE

abierto las 24 horas del día	24-hour service
botiquín	first-aid box
casa de socorro	emergency first-aid centre
comisaría	police station
farmacia de guardia	duty chemist
fuego	fire
guardia civil de tráfico	traffic police
marque …	dial …
policía	police
primeros auxilios	first-aid post
puesto de socorro	first-aid post
servicios de rescate	mountain rescue
socorrista	lifeguard
taller (de reparaciones)	garage
urgencias	casualty department

THINGS YOU'LL HEAR

¿Cuál es su dirección?
What's your address?

¿Dónde se encuentra usted ahora?
Where are you?

¿Puede describirlo/discribirle?
Can you describe it/him?

HEALTH

Under EC Social Security regulations visitors from the UK qualify for free medical treatment on the same basis as the Spanish themselves. If you want to make sure of being in possession of all necessary documentation, you should obtain a T4 from a main post office, fill in the attached E111 and get it stamped at the post office before travelling. With the E111, you'll also get a leaflet explaining how to obtain treatment.

Medicines and drugs are available only from the **farmacia** (chemist's), usually open from 9 am to 1 pm and from 4 pm to 8 pm. If the chemist's is closed, there'll be a notice on the door that gives the address of the **farmacia de guardia** – duty chemist. (See also EMERGENCIES page 108).

USEFUL WORDS AND PHRASES

accident	un accidente	*akthee-denteh*
ambulance	una ambulancia	*amboolanth-ya*
anaemic	anémico	*anneh-meekoh*
appendicitis	una apendicitis	*apendee-theeteess*
appendix	el apéndice	*apen-deetheh*
aspirin	una aspirina	*asspee-reena*
asthma	asma	*azma*
backache	un dolor de espalda	*dolor deh esspalda*
bandage	el vendaje	*vendah-Heh*
bite *(by dog)*	una mordedura	*mordeh-doora*
(by insect)	una picadura	*peeka-doora*
bladder	la vejiga	*veh-Heega*
blister	una ampolla	*ampoh-ya*
blood	la sangre	*sangreh*
blood donor	un donante de sangre	*doh-nanteh deh sangreh*
burn	una quemadura	*keh-madoora*
cancer	el cáncer	*kanthair*

113

chemist	la farmacia	*farm__a__th-ya*
chest	el pecho	*p__eh__-tchoh*
chickenpox	la varicela	*varee-th__eh__-la*
cold	un resfriado	*ressfree-__ah__-doh*
concussion	una conmoción	*konmoth-y__o__n*
constipation	estreñimiento	*estren-yeem-y__e__ntoh*
contact lenses	las lentes de contacto	*l__e__ntess deh kont__a__ktoh*
corn	un callo	*k__a__h-yoh*
cough	tos	*toss*
cut	una cortadura	*korta-d__oo__ra*
dentist	el dentista	*dent__ee__sta*
diabetes	la diabetes	*dee-ab__eh__-tess*
diarrhoea	una diarrea	*dee-arr__eh__-a*
dizzy	mareado	*marr__eh__-__ah__-doh*
doctor	el médico	*m__e__ddeekoh*
earache	un dolor de oídos	*dol__o__r deh oh-__ee__doss*
fever	la fiebre	*fee-__eh__-breh*
filling	un empaste	*emp__a__steh*
first aid	primeros auxilios	*preem__eh__-ross owk-z__ee__l-yoss*
flu	la gripe	*gr__ee__peh*
fracture	una fractura	*frakt__oo__ra*
German measles	la rubeola	*roobeh-__o__la*
glasses	las gafas	*g__a__h-fass*
haemorrhage	una hemorragia	*emmora__H__-ya*
hayfever	la fiebre del heno	*fee-__eh__-breh del __eh__-noh*
headache	un dolor de cabeza	*dol__o__r deh kab__eh__-tha*
heart	el corazón	*korrath__o__n*
heart attack	un infarto	*eemf__a__rtoh*
hospital	el hospital	*osspeet__a__l*
ill	enfermo	*emf__ai__rmoh*
indigestion	una indigestión	*eendee-Hest-y__o__n*
injection	una inyección	*eenyekth-y__o__n*
itch	un picor	*peek__o__r*
kidney	el riñón	*reen-y__o__n*
lump	un bulto	*b__oo__ltoh*

measles	el sarampión	*saramp-yon*
migraine	una jaqueca	*Hakeh-ka*
mumps	las paperas	*papeh-rass*
nausea	náuseas	*now-seh-ass*
nurse *(female)*	la enfermera	*emfairmeh-ra*
(male)	el ATS	*ah-teh-eh-seh*
operation	una operación	*oppeh-rath-yon*
optician	el oculista	*okooleess-ta*
pain	un dolor	*dolor*
penicillin	la penicilina	*peneethee-leena*
plaster *(sticky)*	una tirita	*teereeta*
plaster of Paris	la escayola	*eskayoh-la*
pneumonia	una neumonía	*neh-oomonee-a*
pregnant	embarazada	*embarra-thah-da*
prescription	una receta	*reh-theh-ta*
rheumatism	el reúma	*reh-oo-ma*
scald	una quemadura	*keh-madoora*
scratch	un arañazo	*arran-yah-thoh*
smallpox	la viruela	*veer-weh-la*
sore throat	un dolor de garganta	*dolor deh garganta*
splinter	una astilla	*astee-ya*
sprain	una torcedura	*tortheh-doora*
sting	una picadura	*peeka-doora*
stomach	el estómago	*estoh-magoh*
tonsils	las amígdalas	*ameegda-lass*
toothache	un dolor de muelas	*dolor deh mweh-lass*
travel sickness	mareo	*marreh-oh*
ulcer	una úlcera	*ooltheh-ra*
vaccination	la vacunación	*vakoonath-yon*
vomit	vomitar	*vommee-tar*
whooping cough	la tosferina	*tossfeh-reena*

I have a pain in …
Me duele …
meh dweh-leh

115

I do not feel well
No me encuentro bien
noh meh enkwen-troh byen

I feel faint
Me encuentro débil
meh enkwen-troh deh-beel

I feel sick
Tengo náuseas
teng-goh now-seh-ass

I feel dizzy
Estoy mareado
estoy marreh-ah-doh

It hurts here
Me duele aquí
meh dweh-leh akee

It's a sharp pain
Es un dolor agudo
ess oon dolor agoodoh

It's a dull pain
Es un dolor sordo
ess oon dolor sor-doh

It hurts all the time
Es un dolor constante
ess oon dolor konstanteh

It only hurts now and then
Sólo me duele a ratos
soloh meh dweh-leh a rah-toss

It hurts when you touch it
Me duele al tocarlo
meh dweh-leh al tokarloh

It hurts more at night
Me duele más por la noche
meh dweh-leh mass por la notcheh

It stings/It itches
Me escuece/Me pica
meh ess-kweh-theh/meh peeka

It aches
Me duele
meh dweh-leh

I have a temperature
Tengo fiebre
teng-goh fee-eh-breh

I need a prescription for ...
Necesito una receta para ...
netheh-seetoh oona reh-theh-ta parra

I normally take ...
Normalmente tomo ...
normalmenteh toh-moh

I'm allergic to ...
Soy alérgico a ...
soy allair-Heekoh a

Have you got anything for ...?
¿Tiene usted algo para ...?
tyeh-neh oosteh algoh parra

Do I need a prescription for ...?
¿Hace falta receta para ...?
ah-theh falta reh-theh-ta parra

I have lost a filling
Se me ha caído un empaste
seh meh a ka-eedoh oon empasteh

Will he/she be all right?
¿Estará bien?
estara byen

Will he/she need an operation?
¿Va a necesitar una operación?
ba a nethessee-tar oona oppeh-rath-yon

How is he/she?
¿Cómo está?
koh-moh esta

THINGS YOU'LL SEE

análisis clínicos	clinical tests
casa de socorro	first-aid centre
clínica dental	dental clinic
consulta	surgery
farmacia de guardia	duty chemist
ginecólogo	gynaecologist
médico	doctor
médico general	G.P.
oculista	optician
otorrinolaringólogo	ear, nose and throat specialist
pediatra	pediatrician
primeros auxilios	first-aid centre
sala de espera	waiting room
test del embarazo	pregnancy tests
tomamos la tensión	take your blood pressure
urgencias	emergencies

THINGS YOU'LL HEAR

Tome usted ... comprimidos/pastillas cada vez
Take ... pills/tablets at a time

Con agua
With water

Mastíquelos
Chew them

Una vez/dos veces/tres veces al día
Once/twice/three times a day

Al acostarse
Only when you go to bed

¿Qué toma normalmente?
What do you normally take?

Debería consultar a un médico
I think you should see a doctor

Lo siento, no lo tenemos
I'm sorry, we don't have that

Hace falta una receta médica para eso
For that you need a prescription

CONVERSION TABLES

DISTANCES

A mile is 1.6km. To convert kilometres to miles, divide the km by 8 and multiply by 5. Convert miles to km by dividing the miles by 5 and multiplying by 8.

miles		0.62	1.24	1.86	2.43	3.11	3.73	4.35	6.21
miles *or* km	**1**	**2**	**3**	**4**	**5**	**6**	**7**	**10**
km		1.61	3.22	4.83	6.44	8.05	9.66	11.27	16.10

WEIGHTS

The kilogram is equivalent to 2lb 3oz. To convert kg to lbs, divide by 5 and multiply by 11. One ounce is about 28 grams, and eight ounces about 227 grams; 1lb is therefore about 454 grams.

lbs		2.20	4.41	6.61	8.82	11.02	13.23	19.84	22.04
lbs *or* kg	**1**	**2**	**3**	**4**	**5**	**6**	**9**	**10**
kg		0.45	0.91	1.36	1.81	2.27	2.72	4.08	4.53

TEMPERATURE

To convert Celsius degrees into Fahrenheit, the accurate method is to multiply the °C figure by 1.8 and add 32. Similarly, to convert °F to °C, subtract 32 from the °F figure and divide by 1.8.

°C	-10	0	5	10	20	30	36.9	40	100
°F	14	32	41	50	68	77	98.4	104	212

LIQUIDS

A litre is about 1.75 pints; a gallon is roughly 4.5 litres.

gals		0.22	0.44	1.10	2.20	4.40	6.60	11.00
gals *or* litres	**1**	**2**	**5**	**10**	**20**	**30**	**50**
litres		4.54	9.10	22.73	45.46	90.92	136.4	227.3

TYRE PRESSURES

lb/sq in	18	20	22	24	26	28	30	33
kg/sq cm	1.3	1.4	1.5	1.7	1.8	2.0	2.1	2.3

MINI-DICTIONARY

*Where two forms of nouns or pronouns are given in the Spanish, the first is masculine and the second feminine, eg '**they** ellos/ellas', '**this one** éste/ésta'.*

There are two verbs 'to be' in Spanish: 'ser' is used to describe a permanent condition, such as nationality and occupation, and 'estar' is used to describe a temporary condition. Both forms are given in this order in the dictionary.

a un/una *(see p 5)*
about: about 16 alrededor de dieciséis
accelerator el acelerador
accident el accidente
accommodation el alojamiento
ache el dolor
adaptor el adaptador
address la dirección
adhesive el pegamento
after ... después de ...
aftershave el after-shave
again otra vez
against contra
agency el agente
Aids el Sida
air el aire
air-conditioning el aire acondicionado
aircraft el avión
airline la compañía aérea
airport el aeropuerto
airport bus el autobús del aeropuerto
aisle el pasillo
alarm clock el despertador
alcohol el alcohol
Algeria Argelia
all todo

all the streets todas las calles
that's all eso es todo
almost casi
alone solo
already ya
always siempre
am: I am soy/estoy
ambulance la ambulancia
America América
American *(man)* el americano
(woman) la americana
(adj) americano
and y; *(before word beginning with 'i' or 'hi')* e
ankle el tobillo
another otro
anti-freeze el anticongelante
antiseptic el antiséptico
apartment el apartamento
aperitif el aperitivo
appetite el apetito
apple la manzana
application form el impreso de solicitud
appointment *(business)* la cita
(at hairdresser's) hora
apricot el albaricoque
are: you are es/está
(familiar) eres/estás

we are somos/estamos
they are son/están
arm el brazo
arrive llegar
art el arte
art gallery la galería de arte
artist el/la artista
as: as soon as possible lo antes
posible
ashtray el cenicero
asleep: he's asleep está dormido
aspirin la aspirina
at: at the post office en Correos
at night por la noche
at 3 o'clock a las tres
Atlantic Ocean el Océano
Atlántico
attractive *(person)* guapo
(object) bonito
(offer) atractivo
aunt la tía
Australia Australia
Australian *(man)* el australiano
(woman) la australiana
(adj) australiano
automatic automático
away: is it far away? ¿está lejos?
go away! ¡lárguese!
awful horrible
axe el hacha
axle el eje

baby el niño pequeño, el bebé
back *(not front)* la parte de atrás
(body) la espalda
to come back volver
bacon el bacon
bacon and eggs huevos fritos con
bacon
bad malo
bag la bolsa
bait el cebo
bake cocer al horno
bakery la panadería

balcony el balcón
Balearic Islands las (Islas) Baleares
ball la pelota
banana el plátano
band *(musicians)* la banda
bandage la venda
bank el banco
banknote el billete de banco
bar *(drinks)* el bar
bar of chocolate una tableta de
chocolate
barbecue la barbacoa
barber's la peluquería de caballeros
bargain la ganga
basement el sótano
basin *(sink)* el lavabo
basket el cesto
bath el baño
to have a bath darse un baño
bathroom el cuarto de baño
battery *(car)* la batería
(torch etc) la pila
Bay of Biscay el Golfo de Vizcaya
beach la playa
beach ball el balón de playa
beans las judías
beard la barba
beautiful *(object)* precioso
(person) guapo
because porque
bed la cama
bed linen la ropa de cama
bedroom el dormitorio
beef la carne de vaca
beer la cerveza
before ... antes de ...
beginner un/una principiante
behind ... detrás de ...
beige beige
bell *(church)* la campana
(door) el timbre
below ... debajo de ...
belt el cinturón
beside al lado de

best (el) mejor
better mejor
between ... entre ...
bicycle la bicicleta
big grande
bill la cuenta
bin liner la bolsa de basura
bird el pájaro
Biro ® el bolígrafo
birthday el cumpleaños
   happy birthday! ¡felicidades!
birthday present el regalo de
   cumpleaños
biscuit la galleta
bite *(noun: by dog)* la mordedura
   (by insect) la picadura
   (verb: by dog) morder
   (by insect) picar
bitter amargo
black negro
blackberries las moras
blackcurrants las grosellas negras
blanket la manta
bleach *(noun)* la lejía
   (verb: hair) teñir
blind *(cannot see)* ciego
blinds las persianas
blister una ampolla
blizzard la ventisca
blond(e) *(adj)* rubio
blood la sangre
blouse la blusa
blue azul
boat el barco
   (small) la barca
body el cuerpo
boil *(of water)* hervir
   (egg etc) cocer
bolt *(noun: on door)* el cerrojo
   (verb) echar el cerrojo
bone el hueso
bonnet *(car)* el capó
book *(noun)* el libro
   (verb) reservar

bookshop la librería
boot *(car)* el maletero
   (footwear) la bota
border el borde
   (between countries) la frontera
boring aburrido
born: I was born in ... nací en ...
both: both of them los dos
   both of us los dos
   both ... and ... tanto ... como ...
bottle la botella
bottle-opener el abrebotellas
bottom el fondo
   (part of body) el trasero
bowl el cuenco
box la caja
box office la taquilla
boy el chico
boyfriend el novio
bra el sostén
bracelet la pulsera
braces los tirantes
brake *(noun)* el freno
   (verb) frenar
brandy el coñac
bread el pan
breakdown *(car)* la avería
   (nervous) la crisis nerviosa
   I've had a breakdown *(car)* he
   tenido una avería
breakfast el desayuno
breathe respirar
bridge el puente
   (game) el bridge
briefcase la cartera
British británico
brochure el folleto
broken roto
brooch el broche
brother el hermano
brown marrón
   (hair) castaño
   (skin) moreno
bruise el cardenal

brush *(noun: hair)* el cepillo del pelo
  (paint) la brocha
  (for cleaning) el cepillo
  (verb: hair) cepillar el pelo
bucket el cubo
building el edificio
bull el toro
bullfight la corrida de toros
bullfighter el torero
bullring la plaza de toros
bumper el parachoques
burglar el ladrón
burn *(noun)* la quemadura
  (verb) quemar
bus el autobús
business el negocio
  it's none of your business no es asunto suyo
bus station la estación de autobuses
busy *(occupied)* ocupado
  (bar) concurrido
but pero
butcher's la carnicería
butter la mantequilla
button el botón
buy comprar
by: by the window junto a la ventana
  by Friday para el viernes
  by myself yo solo
  written by ... escrito por ...

cabbage la col
cable car el teleférico
café el café
cagoule el chubasquero
cake *(small)* el pastel
  (large) la tarta
  sponge cake el bizcocho
calculator la calculadora
call: what's it called? ¿cómo se llama?
camcorder la videocámara

camera la máquina de fotos
campsite el camping
camshaft el árbol de levas
can *(tin)* la lata
can: can you ...? ¿puede ...?
  I can't ... no puedo ...
Canada Canadá
Canadian el/la canadiense
  (adj) canadiense
canal el canal
Canaries las (Islas) Canarias
candle la vela
cap *(bottle)* el tapón
  (hat) la gorra
car el coche
caravan la caravana
carburettor el carburador
card la tarjeta
cardigan la rebeca
careful prudente
  be careful! ¡cuidado!
caretaker el portero, el encargado
carpet la alfombra
carriage *(train)* el vagón
carrot la zanahoria
carry-cot el capazo
case *(suitcase)* la maleta
cash *(noun)* el dinero
  (verb) cobrar
  to pay cash pagar al contado
cash dispenser el cajero automático
cassette la cassette, la cinta
cassette player el cassette
castanets unas castañuelas
Castile Castilla
Castilian castellano
castle el castillo
cat el gato
Catalonia Cataluña
cathedral la catedral
Catholic *(adj)* católico
cauliflower la coliflor
cave la cueva
cemetery el cementerio

central heating la calefacción
central
centre el centro
certificate el certificado
chair la silla
change *(noun: money)* el cambio
(verb: money) cambiar
(clothes) cambiarse
(trains etc) hacer transbordo
cheap barato
check-in *(desk)* (el mostrador de)
facturación
check in *(verb)* facturar
cheers! *(toast)* ¡salud!
cheese el queso
chemist's la farmacia
cheque el cheque
cheque book el talonario de
cheques
cheque card la tarjeta de banco
cherry la cereza
chess el adjedrez
chest *(part of body)* el pecho
(furniture) el arcón
chest of drawers la cómoda
chewing gum el chicle
chicken el pollo
child el niño
(female) la niña
children los niños
china la porcelana
chips las patatas fritas
chocolate el chocolate
box of chocolates una caja de
bombones
chop *(food)* la chuleta
(verb: cut) cortar
Christian name el nombre de pila
church la iglesia
cigar el puro
cigarette el cigarrillo
cinema el cine
city la ciudad
city centre el centro (urbano)

class la clase
classical music la música clásica
clean *(adj)* limpio
clear *(obvious)* evidente
(water) claro
clever listo
cling film el plástico para envolver
clock el reloj
close *(near)* cerca
(stuffy) sofocante
(verb) cerrar
closed cerrado
clothes la ropa
clubs *(cards)* tréboles
coach el autobús
(of train) el vagón
coach station la estación de
autobuses
coat el abrigo
coathanger la percha
cockroach la cucaracha
coffee el café
coin la moneda
cold *(illness)* un resfriado
(adj) frío
I have a cold tengo un resfriado
I am cold tengo frío
collar el cuello
(of animal) el collar
collection *(stamps etc)* la colección
(postal) la recogida
colour el color
colour film la película en color
comb *(noun)* el peine
(verb) peinar
come venir
I come from ... soy de ...
we came last week llegamos la
semana pasada
come here! ¡venga aquí!
Common Market el Mercado
Común
compact disc el disco compacto
compartment el compartimento

complicated complicado
computer el ordenador
concert el concierto
conditioner *(hair)* el acondicionador
condom el condón
conductor *(bus)* el cobrador
(orchestra) el director
congratulations! ¡enhorabuena! •
consulate el consulado
contact lenses las lentes de contacto
contraceptive el anticonceptivo
cook *(noun)* el cocinero
(female) la cocinera
(verb) guisar
cooker la cocina
cooking utensils los utensilios de cocina
cool fresco
cork el corcho
corkscrew el sacacorchos
corner *(of street)* la esquina
(of room) el rincón
corridor el pasillo
cosmetics los cosméticos
cost *(verb)* costar
what does it cost? ¿cuánto cuesta?
cotton el algodón
cotton wool el algodón
cough *(noun)* la tos
(verb) toser
country *(state)* el país
(not town) el campo
cousin el primo
(female) la prima
crab el cangrejo
cramp el calambre
crayfish las cigalas
cream *(dairy)* la nata
(lotion) la crema
credit card la tarjeta de crédito
crisps las patatas fritas

crowded lleno
cruise el crucero
crutches las muletas
cry *(weep)* llorar
(shout) gritar
cucumber el pepino
cufflinks los gemelos
cup la taza
cupboard el armario
curlers los rulos
curls los rizos
curry el curry
curtain la cortina
Customs la Aduana
cut *(noun)* la cortadura
(verb) cortar

dad papá
damp húmedo
dance *(noun)* el baile
(verb) bailar
dangerous peligroso
dark oscuro
dark blue azul oscuro
daughter la hija
day el día
dead muerto
deaf sordo
dear *(person)* querido
(expensive) caro
deckchair la tumbona
deep profundo
delayed retrasado
deliberately a propósito
dentist el/la dentista
dentures la dentadura postiza
deny negar
deodorant el desodorante
department store los grandes almacenes
departure la salida
departure lounge salidas
develop *(film)* revelar
diamonds *(jewels)* los diamantes

(cards) diamantes
diarrhoea la diarrea
diary la agenda
dictionary el diccionario
die morir
diesel *(oil)* fuel-oil
   (adj: engine) diesel
different diferente
  that's different! ¡eso es distinto!
  I'd like a different one quería
  otro distinto
difficult difícil
dining room el comedor
directory *(telephone)* la guía
  telefónica
dirty sucio
disabled minusválido
disposable nappies pañales
  desechables
distributor *(car)* el distribuidor
divorced divorciado
do hacer
  how do you do? ¿qué tal?
doctor el médico
  (female) la médica
document el documento
dog el perro
doll la muñeca
dollar el dólar
door la puerta
double room la habitación doble
doughnut el dónut ®
down hacia abajo
drawing pin la chincheta
dress el vestido
drink *(noun)* la bebida
  (verb) beber
  would you like a drink? ¿quiere
  beber algo?
drinking water agua potable
drive *(verb)* conducir
driver el conductor
driving licence el carnet de
  conducir

drunk borracho
dry seco
  (sherry) fino
dummy *(for baby)* el chupete
during durante
dustbin el cubo de la basura
duster el trapo del polvo
duty-free libre de impuestos
  duty-free shop el duty-free
duvet el edredón

each *(every)* cada
  300 pesetas each trescientas
  pesetas cada uno
ear *(inner)* el oído
  (outer) la oreja
  ears las orejas
early temprano
earrings los pendientes
east el Este
easy fácil
eat comer
EC la CE
egg el huevo
either: either of them cualquiera de
  ellos
  either ... or ... o bien ... o ...
elastic elástico
elastic band la goma
elbow el codo
electric eléctrico
electricity la electricidad
else: something else algo más
  someone else alguien más
  somewhere else en otro sitio
embarrassing embarazoso
embassy la embajada
embroidery el bordado
emergency la emergencia
emergency brake *(train)* el freno de
  emergencia
emergency exit la salida de
  emergencia
empty vacío

end el final
engaged *(couple)* prometido
  (occupied) ocupado
engine *(motor)* el motor
England Inglaterra
English inglés
Englishman el inglés
Englishwoman la inglesa
enlargement la ampliación
enough bastante
entertainment las diversiones
entrance la entrada
envelope el sobre
escalator la escalera mecánica
especially sobre todo
evening la tarde
every cada
  every day todos los días
everyone todos
everything todo
everywhere por todas partes
example el ejemplo
  for example por ejemplo
excellent excelente
excess baggage exceso de equipaje
exchange *(verb)* cambiar
exchange rate el cambio
excursion la excursión
excuse me! *(to get attention)* ¡oiga,
  por favor!
  (when sneezing etc) ¡perdón!
  excuse me please *(to get past)*
  ¿me hace el favor?
exit la salida
expensive caro
extension lead el cable alargador
eye el ojo

face la cara
faint *(unclear)* tenue
  (verb) desmayarse
fair *(noun)* la feria
  it's not fair no hay derecho
false teeth la dentadura postiza

family la familia
fan *(ventilator)* el ventilador
  (handheld) el abanico
  (enthusiast) el fan
  (football) el hincha
fantastic fantástico
far lejos
  how far is it to ...? ¿qué distancia
  hay a ...?
fare el billete
farm la granja
farmer el granjero
fashion la moda
fast rápido
fat *(person)* gordo
  (on meat etc) la grasa
father el padre
fax *(noun)* el fax
  (verb: document) enviar por fax
feel *(touch)* tocar
  I feel hot tengo calor
  I feel like ... me apetece ...
  I don't feel well no me encuentro
  bien
felt-tip pen el rotulador
fence la cerca
ferry el ferry
fiancé el prometido
fiancée la prometida
field el campo
fig el higo
filling *(in tooth)* el empaste
  (in sandwich, cake) el relleno
film la película
filter el filtro
filter papers los papeles de filtro
finger el dedo
fire el fuego
  (blaze) el incendio
fire extinguisher el extintor
fireworks los fuegos artificiales
first primero
  first aid primeros auxilios
  first floor el primer piso

fish el pez
(food) el pescado
fishing la pesca
  to go fishing ir a pescar
fishmonger's la pescadería
fizzy con gas
flag la bandera
flash *(camera)* el flash
flat *(apartment)* el piso
  (level) plano
flavour el sabor
flea la pulga
flight el vuelo
floor el suelo
  (storey) el piso
flour la harina
flower la flor
flute la flauta
fly *(insect)* la mosca
  (verb: of plane, insect) volar
  (of person) viajar en avión
fog la niebla
folk music la música folklórica
food la comida
food poisoning la intoxicación
  alimenticia
foot el pie
football *(game)* el fútbol
  (ball) el balón
for: for me para mí
  what for? ¿para qué?
  for a week (para) una semana
foreigner el extranjero
  (female) la extranjera
forest el bosque
  (tropical) la selva
forget olvidar
fork el tenedor
fortnight la quincena
fountain pen la (pluma)
  estilográfica
fourth cuarto
France Francia
free *(not engaged)* libre

(no charge) gratis
freezer el congelador
French francés
fridge el frigorífico
friend el amigo
  (female) la amiga
friendly simpático
fringe *(hair)* el flequillo
front: in front of ... delante de ...
frost la escarcha
fruit la fruta
fruit juice el zumo de frutas
fry freír
frying pan la sartén
full lleno
  I'm full (up) estoy lleno
full board pensión completa
funny divertido
  (odd) raro
furniture los muebles

garage *(for parking)* el garage
  (for repairs) el taller
garden el jardín
garlic el ajo
gas-permeable lenses las lentes de
  contacto semi-rígidas
gate la puerta
  (at airport) la puerta de embarque
gay gay
gear lever la palanca de velocidades
gel *(hair)* el gel
gents *(toilet)* los servicios de caballeros
German alemán
Germany Alemania
get *(fetch)* traer
  have you got ...? ¿tiene ...?
  to get the train coger el tren
get back: we get back tomorrow
  nos volvemos mañana
  to get something back recobrar
  algo
get in *(of train etc)* subirse
  (of person) llegar

get off *(bus etc)* bajarse
get on *(bus etc)* subirse
get out bajarse
   (bring out) sacar
get up *(rise)* levantarse
Gibraltar Gibraltar
gift el regalo
gin la ginebra
ginger *(spice)* el jengibre
girl la chica
girlfriend la novia
give dar
glad alegre
glass *(material)* el cristal
   (for drinking) el vaso
glasses las gafas
gloss prints las copias con brillo
gloves los guantes
glue el pegamento
go ir
gold el oro
good bueno
   good! ¡bien!
goodbye adiós
government el gobierno
granddaughter la nieta
grandfather el abuelo
grandmother la abuela
grandparents los abuelos
grandson el nieto
grapes las uvas
grass la hierba
Great Britain Gran Bretaña
green verde
grey gris
grill la parrilla
grocer's la tienda de comestibles
ground floor la planta baja
groundsheet la lona impermeable
guarantee *(noun)* la garantía
   (verb) garantizar
guide el/la guía
guide book la guía turística
guitar la guitarra

gun *(rifle)* la escopeta
   (pistol) la pistola

hair el pelo
haircut el corte de pelo
hairdresser's la peluquería
hair dryer el secador (de pelo)
hair spray la laca
half medio
   half an hour media hora
half board media pensión
ham el jamón
hamburger la hamburguesa
hammer el martillo
hand la mano
handbag el bolso
handbrake el freno de mano
handkerchief el pañuelo
handle *(door)* el picaporte
handsome guapo
hangover la resaca
happy contento
harbour el puerto
hard duro
   (difficult) difícil
hard lenses las lentes de contacto
duras
hardware shop la ferretería
hat el sombrero
   (woollen) el gorro
have tener
   I don't have ... no tengo ...
   have you got ...? ¿tiene ...?
   I have to go tengo que irme
   can I have ...? ¿me da ...?
hayfever la fiebre del heno
he él
head la cabeza
headache el dolor de cabeza
hear oír
hearing aid el audífono
heart el corazón
hearts *(cards)* corazones
heater la estufa

heating la calefacción
heavy pesado
heel el talón
  (shoe) el tacón
hello hola
  (on phone) dígame
help *(noun)* la ayuda
  (verb) ayudar
her: it's her es ella
  it's for her es para ella
  give it to her déselo
  her book su libro
  her shoes sus zapatos
  it's hers es suyo
hi! ¡hola!
high alto
highway code el código de la
  circulación
hill el monte
him: it's him es él
  it's for him es para él
  give it to him déselo
hire alquilar
his: his book su libro
  his shoes sus zapatos
  it's his es suyo
history la historia
hitchhike hacer auto-stop
hobby el hobby
holidays las vacaciones
home: at home en casa
honest honrado
  (sincere) sincero
honey la miel
honeymoon el viaje de novios
horn *(car)* el claxon
  (animal) el cuerno
horrible horrible
hospital el hospital
hour la hora
house la casa
hovercraft el aerodeslizador
how? ¿cómo?
hungry: I'm hungry tengo
  hambre
hurry: I'm in a hurry tengo prisa
husband el marido
hydrofoil la hidroaleta

I yo
ice el hielo
ice cream el helado
ice lolly el polo
ice skates los patines para hielo
if si
ignition el encendido
ill enfermo
immediately inmediatamente
impossible imposible
in en
  in English en inglés
  in the hotel en el hotel
  in Barcelona en Barcelona
  he's not in no está
infection la infección
information la información
injection la inyección
injury la herida
ink la tinta
inn la fonda
inner tube la cámara (neumática)
insect el insecto
insect repellent la loción anti-
  mosquitos
insomnia el insomnio
instant coffee el café instantáneo
insurance el seguro
interesting interesante
interpret interpretar
interpreter el/la intérprete
invitation la invitación
Ireland Irlanda
Irish irlandés
Irishman el irlandés
Irishwoman la irlandesa
iron *(material)* el hierro
  (for clothes) la plancha
  (verb) planchar

is es/está
island la isla
it lo/la
Italian *(adj)* italiano
Italy Italia
its su

jacket la chaqueta
jam la mermelada
jazz el jazz
jeans los tejanos, los vaqueros
jellyfish la medusa
jeweller's la joyería
job el trabajo
jog *(verb)* hacer footing
joke la broma
   (story) el chiste
journey el viaje
jumper el jersey
just *(only)* sólo
   it's just arrived acaba de llegar

kettle el hervidor de agua
key la llave
kidney el riñón
kilo el kilo
kilometre el kilómetro
kitchen la cocina
knee la rodilla
knife el cuchillo
knit hacer punto
knitwear artículos de punto
know saber
   (person, place) conocer
   I don't know no sé

label la etiqueta
lace el encaje
laces *(of shoe)* los cordones (de los
   zapatos)
ladies *(toilet)* los servicios de señoras
lady la señora
lake el lago
lamb el cordero

lamp la lámpara
lampshade la pantalla
land *(noun)* la tierra
   (verb) aterrizar
language el idioma
large grande
last *(final)* último
   last week la semana pasada
   at last! ¡por fin!
late: it's getting late se está
   haciendo tarde
   the bus is late el autobús se ha
   retrasado
later más tarde
laugh reír
launderette la lavandería automática
laundry *(dirty)* la ropa sucia
   (washed) la colada
laxative el laxante
lazy perezoso
leaf la hoja
leaflet el folleto
learn aprender
leather el cuero
left *(not right)* izquierdo
   there's nothing left no queda
   nada
left-luggage locker la consigna
leg la pierna
lemon el limón
lemonade la limonada
length la longitud
lens la lente
less menos
lesson la clase
letter *(post)* la carta
   (of alphabet) la letra
lettuce la lechuga
library la biblioteca
licence el permiso
life la vida
lift *(in building)* el ascensor
   could you give me a lift? ¿me
   podría llevar en su coche?

light *(noun)* la luz
  (adj: not heavy) ligero
  (not dark) claro
light bulb la bombilla
light meter el fotómetro
lighter el encendedor
lighter fuel el gas para el
  encendedor
like: I like it me gusta
  I like swimming me gusta nadar
  it's like ... es como ...
  like this one como éste
lime *(fruit)* la lima
lip salve la crema labial
lipstick la barra de labios
liqueur el licor
list la lista
litre el litro
litter la basura
little *(small)* pequeño
  it's a little big es un poco grande
  just a little sólo un poquito
liver el hígado
lobster la langosta
lollipop el chupa-chups
long largo
lorry el camión
lost property office la oficina de
  objetos perdidos
lot: a lot mucho
loud alto
lounge *(in house)* el cuarto de estar
  (in hotel etc) el salón
love *(noun)* el amor
  (verb) querer
  I love Spain me encanta España
lover el/la amante
low bajo
luck la suerte
  good luck! ¡suerte!
luggage el equipaje
luggage rack la rejilla de equipajes
lunch la comida

mad loco
magazine la revista
mail el correo
Majorca Mallorca
make hacer
make-up el maquillaje
man el hombre
manager el/la gerente
  (hotel: male) el director
  (female) la directora
many: not many no muchos
map el mapa
  a map of Madrid un plano de
  Madrid
marble el mármol
margarine la margarina
market el mercado
marmalade la mermelada de naranja
married casado
mascara el rímel
mass *(church)* la misa
match *(light)* la cerilla
  (sport) el partido
material *(cloth)* la tela
matter: it doesn't matter no
  importa
mattress el colchón
maybe quizás
me: it's me soy yo
  it's for me es para mí
  give it to me démelo
meal la comida
mean: what does this mean? ¿qué
  significa esto?
meat la carne
mechanic el mecánico
medicine la medicina
Mediterranean el Mediterráneo
medium *(sherry)* amontillado
medium-dry *(wine)* semi-seco
meeting la reunión
melon el melón
menu la carta
  set menu el menú (del día)

133

message el recado
midday mediodía
middle: in the middle en el centro
midnight medianoche
milk la leche
mine: it's mine es mío
mineral water el agua mineral
minute el minuto
mirror el espejo
Miss Señorita
mistake la equivocación
money el dinero
month el mes
monument el monumento
moon la luna
moped el ciclomotor
more más
morning la mañana
in the morning por la mañana
Morocco Marruecos
mosaic el mosaico
mosquito el mosquito
mother la madre
motorbike la motocicleta
motorboat la motora
motorway la autopista
mountain la montaña
mountain bike la bicicleta de montaña
mouse el ratón
mousse *(for hair)* la mousse
moustache el bigote
mouth la boca
move *(verb: something)* mover
(onself) moverse
(house) mudarse (de casa)
don't move! ¡no se mueva!
movie la película
Mr Señor
Mrs Señora
much: much better mucho mejor
much slower mucho más despacio

mug la jarrita
mum mamá
museum el museo
mushroom la seta
music la música
musical instrument el instrumento musical
musician el músico
mussels los mejillones
must: I must ... tengo que ...
mustard la mostaza
my: my book mi libro
my keys mis llaves

nail *(metal)* el clavo
(finger) la uña
nail clippers el cortauñas
nail file la lima de uñas
nail polish el esmalte de uñas
name el nombre
what's your name? ¿cómo se llama usted?
nappy el pañal
narrow estrecho
near: near the door junto a la puerta
near London cerca de Londres
necessary necesario
neck el cuello
necklace el collar
need *(verb)* necesitar
I need ... necesito ...
there's no need no hace falta
needle la aguja
negative *(photo)* el negativo
neither: neither of them ninguno de ellos
neither ... nor ... ni ... ni ...
nephew el sobrino
never nunca
new nuevo
news las noticias
newsagent el kiosko de periódicos
newspaper el periódico

New Zealand Nueva Zelanda
New Zealander *(man)* el
  neozelandés
  (woman) la neozelandesa
  (adj) neozelandés
next siguiente
  next week la semana que viene
  what next? ¿y ahora qué?
nice bonito
  (pleasant) agradable
  (to eat) bueno
niece la sobrina
night la noche
nightclub la discoteca
nightdress el camisón
night porter el vigilante nocturno
no *(response)* no
  I have no money no tengo
  dinero
nobody nadie
noisy ruidoso
north el norte
Northern Ireland Irlanda del
  Norte
nose la nariz
not no
  he's not ... no es/está ...
notebook el cuaderno
nothing nada
novel la novela
now ahora
nowhere en ninguna parte
nudist el/la nudista
number el número
number plate la matrícula
nut *(fruit)* la nuez
  (for bolt) la tuerca

oars los remos
occasionally de vez en cuando
octopus el pulpo
of de
office *(place)* la oficina
  (room) el despacho

often a menudo
oil el aceite
ointment la pomada
OK vale
old viejo
  how old are you? ¿cuántos años
  tiene?
olive la aceituna
olive oil el aceite de oliva
olive tree el olivo
omelette la tortilla
on ... en ...
one uno
onion la cebolla
only sólo
open *(adj)* abierto
  (verb) abrir
operation la operación
operator la operadora
opposite: opposite the hotel
  enfrente del hotel
optician el oculista
or o
orange *(fruit)* la naranja
  (colour) naranja
orange juice el zumo de naranja
orchestra la orquesta
ordinary corriente
organ *(music)* el órgano
other: the other (one) el otro
our nuestro
  it's ours es nuestro
out: he's out no está
outside fuera
oven el horno
over ... encima de ...
  (more than) más de ...
  it's over the road está al otro lado
  de la calle
  when the party is over cuando
  termine la fiesta
  over there allí
overtake adelantar
oyster la ostra

pack of cards la baraja
package *(parcel)* el paquete
packet el paquete
  (cigarettes) la cajetilla
  (sweets, crisps) la bolsa
padlock el candado
page la página
pain el dolor
paint *(noun)* la pintura
pair el par
palace el palacio
pale pálido
pancakes las crepes
paper el papel
  (newspaper) el periódico
paracetamol el paracetamol
paraffin la parafina
parcel el paquete
pardon? ¿cómo dice?
parents los padres
park *(noun)* el parque
  (verb) aparcar
parsley el perejil
parting *(hair)* la raya
party *(celebration)* la fiesta
  (group) el grupo
  (political) el partido
passenger el pasajero
passport el pasaporte
pasta la pasta
path el camino
pavement la acera
pay pagar
peach el melocotón
peanuts los cacahuetes
pear la pera
pearl la perla
peas los guisantes
pedestrian el peatón
peg *(clothes)* la pinza
  (tent) la estaca
pen la pluma
pencil el lápiz
pencil sharpener el sacapuntas

penfriend el amigo por
correspondencia
  (female) la amiga por
correspondencia
penknife la navaja
people la gente
pepper la pimienta
  (red, green) el pimiento
peppermints las pastillas de menta
per: per night por noche
perfect perfecto
perfume el perfume
perhaps quizás
perm la permanente
petrol la gasolina
petrol station la gasolinera
photograph *(noun)* la foto(grafía)
  (verb) fotografiar
photographer el fotógrafo
phrase book el libro de frases
piano el piano
pickpocket el carterista
picnic el picnic
piece el pedazo
pillow la almohada
pilot el piloto
pin el alfiler
pine *(tree)* el pino
pineapple la piña
pink rosa
pipe *(for smoking)* la pipa
  (for water) la tubería
piston el pistón
pizza la pizza
place el lugar
  at your place en su casa
plant la planta
plaster *(for cut)* la tirita
plastic el plástico
plastic bag la bolsa de plástico
plate el plato
platform el andén
play *(theatre)* la obra de teatro
  (verb) jugar

please por favor
plug *(electrical)* el enchufe
  (sink) el tapón
pocket el bolsillo
poison el veneno
police la policía
policeman el policía
police station la comisaría
politics la política
poor pobre
  (bad quality) malo
pop music la música pop
pork la carne de cerdo
port *(harbour)* el puerto
  (drink) el oporto
porter *(hotel)* el conserje
Portugal Portugal
Portuguese portugués
possible posible
post *(noun)* el correo
  (verb) echar al correo
post box el buzón
postcard la postal
poster el póster
postman el cartero
post office (la oficina de) Correos
potato la patata
poultry las aves
pound *(money)* la libra
  (weight) la libra
powder el polvo
  (make-up) los polvos
pram el cochecito
prawns las gambas
prefer preferir
prescription la receta
pretty bonito
  (quite) bastante
priest el cura
private privado
problem el problema
protection factor el factor de
  protección
public público

pull tirar de
puncture el pinchazo
purple morado
purse el monedero
push empujar
pushchair la sillita de ruedas
put poner
pyjamas el pijama
Pyrenees los Pirineos

quality la calidad
quarter un cuarto
quay el muelle
question la pregunta
queue *(noun)* la cola
  (verb) hacer cola
quick rápido
quiet tranquilo
  (person) callado
quite *(fairly)* bastante
  (fully) completamente

radiator el radiador
radio la radio
radish el rábano
railway el ferrocarril
rain la lluvia
raincoat la gabardina
raisins las pasas
raspberry la frambuesa
rare *(uncommon)* raro
  (steak) poco pasado
rat la rata
razor blades las cuchillas de afeitar
read leer
reading lamp el flexo
  (bedside) la lamparilla de noche
ready listo
receipt el recibo
receptionist el/la recepcionista
record *(music)* el disco
  (sporting etc) el récord
record player el tocadiscos
record shop la tienda de discos

red rojo
  (wine) tinto
refreshments los refrescos
relative el pariente
relax relajarse
  (rest) descansar
religion la religión
remember: I remember me
  recuerdo
  I don't remember no me
  acuerdo
rent *(verb)* alquilar
reservation la reserva
rest *(noun: remainder)* el resto
  (verb: relax) descansar
restaurant el restaurante
restaurant car el vagón-
  restaurante
return *(come back)* volver
  (give back) devolver
return ticket el billete de ida y
  vuelta
rice el arroz
rich rico
right *(correct)* correcto
  (not left) derecho
ring *(verb: phone)* llamar por
  teléfono
  (wedding etc) el anillo
ripe maduro
river el río
road la carretera
rock *(stone)* la roca
  (music) el rock
roll *(bread)* el bollo
roof el tejado
room la habitación
  (space) sitio
rope la cuerda
rose la rosa
round *(circular)* redondo
  it's my round me toca a mí
row *(verb)* remar
rowing boat la barca de remos

rubber *(eraser)* la goma (de borrar)
  (material) la goma
rubbish la basura
ruby *(stone)* el rubí
rucksack la mochila
rug *(mat)* la alfombra
  (blanket) la manta
ruins las ruinas
ruler *(for drawing)* la regla
rum el ron
run *(verb)* correr
runway la pista

sad triste
safe *(not dangerous)* seguro
safety pin el imperdible
sailboard la tabla de windsurfing
sailing boat el balandro
salad la ensalada
sale *(at reduced prices)* las rebajas
salmon el salmón
salt la sal
same: the same dress el mismo
  vestido
  the same people la misma gente
  same again please lo mismo otra
  vez, por favor
sand la arena
sandals las sandalias
sand dunes las dunas
sandwich el bocadillo
sanitary towels las compresas
sauce la salsa
saucepan el cazo
sauna la sauna
sausage la salchicha
say decir
  what did you say? ¿qué ha dicho?
  how do you say ...? ¿cómo se
  dice ...?
scampi las gambas
scarf la bufanda
  (head) el pañuelo
school la escuela

scissors las tijeras
Scotland Escocia
Scotsman el escocés
Scotswoman la escocesa
Scottish escocés
screw el tornillo
screwdriver el destornillador
sea el mar
seafood mariscos
seat el asiento
seat belt el cinturón de seguridad
second el segundo
see ver
  I can't see no veo
  I see comprendo
sell vender
sellotape ® el papel Cello ®
separate *(adj)* distinto
separated separado
serious serio
serviette la servilleta
several varios
sew coser
shampoo el champú
shave *(noun)* un afeitado
  to have a shave afeitarse
shaving foam la espuma de
  afeitar
shawl el chal
she ella
sheet la sábana
  (of paper) la hoja
shell la concha
shellfish mariscos
sherry el jerez
ship el barco
shirt la camisa
shoe laces los cordones de los
  zapatos
shoe polish la crema de zapatos
shoes los zapatos
shop la tienda
shopping la compra
  to go shopping ir de compras

short corto
shorts los pantalones cortos
shoulder el hombro
shower *(bath)* la ducha
  (rain) el chaparrón
shrimps las quisquillas
shutter *(camera)* el obturador
  (window) el postigo
sick: I feel sick tengo náuseas
  to be sick *(vomit)* devolver
side *(edge)* el borde
sidelights las luces de posición
sights: the sights of ... los lugares
  de interés de ...
silk la seda
silver *(metal)* la plata
  (colour) plateado
simple sencillo
sing cantar
single *(one)* único
  (unmarried) soltero
single room la habitación individual
sister la hermana
skid patinar
skiing: to go skiing ir a esquiar
skin cleanser la leche limpiadora
ski resort la estación de esquí
skirt la falda
skis los esquís
sky el cielo
sleep *(noun)* el sueño
  (verb) dormir
sleeper el coche-cama
sleeping bag el saco de dormir
sleeping pill el somnífero
slippers las zapatillas
slow lento
small pequeño
smell *(noun)* el olor
  (verb) oler
smile *(noun)* la sonrisa
  (verb) sonreír
smoke *(noun)* el humo
  (verb) fumar

snack la comida ligera
snow la nieve
so: so good tan bueno
  not so much no tanto
soaking solution *(for contact lenses)*
  la solución limpiadora
soap el jabón
socks los calcetines
soda water la soda
soft lenses las lentes de contacto
  blandas
somebody alguien
somehow de algún modo
something algo
sometimes a veces
somewhere en alguna parte
son el hijo
song la canción
sorry! ¡perdón!
  I'm sorry perdón/lo siento
  sorry? *(pardon)* ¿cómo dice?
soup la sopa
south el sur
South America Sudamérica
souvenir el recuerdo
spade la pala
spades *(cards)* picas
Spain España
Spaniard *(man)* el español
  (woman) la española
Spanish español
  the Spanish los españoles
spanner la llave inglesa
speak hablar
  do you speak ...? ¿habla ...?
  I don't speak ... no hablo ...
speed la velocidad
speed limit el límite de velocidad
spider la araña
spinach las espinacas
spoon la cuchara
spring *(mechanical)* el muelle
  (season) la primavera
square *(noun: in town)* la plaza

  (adj) cuadrado
staircase la escalera
stairs las escaleras
stamp el sello
stapler la grapadora
star la estrella
start *(noun: beginning)* el principio
  (verb) empezar
station la estación
statue la estatua
steak el filete
steal robar
  it's been stolen lo han robado
steamer *(boat)* el vapor
stockings las medias
stomach el estómago
stomach ache el dolor de estómago
stop *(noun: bus)* la parada
  (verb) parar
  stop! ¡alto!
storm la tormenta
strawberries las fresas
stream *(small river)* el arroyo
street la calle
string la cuerda
strong fuerte
student el/la estudiante
stupid estúpido
suburbs las afueras
sugar el azúcar
suit *(noun)* el traje
  it suits you te sienta bien
suitcase la maleta
sun el sol
sunbathe tomar el sol
sunburn la quemadura de sol
sunglasses las gafas de sol
sunny: it's sunny hace sol
sunshade la sombrilla
suntan: to get a suntan broncearse
suntan lotion la loción bronceadora
suntanned bronceado
supermarket el supermercado
supper la cena

supplement el suplemento
sure seguro
surname el apellido
sweat *(noun)* el sudor
  (verb) sudar
sweatshirt la sudadera
sweet *(noun: candy)* el caramelo
  (adj: not sour) dulce
  (sherry) oloroso
swim *(verb)* nadar
swimming costume el bañador, el
  traje de baño
swimming pool la piscina
swimming trunks el bañador
switch el interruptor
synagogue la sinagoga

table la mesa
tablet la pastilla
take tomar
take away: to take away *(food)*
  para llevar
take-off el despegue
talcum powder los polvos de talco
talk *(noun)* la charla
  (verb) hablar
tall alto
tampons los tampones
tangerine la mandarina
tap el grifo
tapestry el tapiz
tea el té
teacher el profesor
  (female) la profesora
tea towel el paño de cocina
telegram el telegrama
telephone *(noun)* el teléfono
  (verb) telefonear
telephone box la cabina telefónica
television la televisión
temperature la temperatura
  (fever) la fiebre
tent la tienda (de campaña)
tent peg la estaquilla

tent pole el mástil
than que
thank *(verb)* agradecer
  thank you gracias
 thanks gracias
that: that one ése/ésa
  that bus ese autobús
  that man ese hombre
  that woman esa mujer
  what's that? ¿qué es eso?
  I think that ... creo que ...
the el/la
  (plural) los/las *(see p 5)*
their: their room su habitación
  their books sus libros
  it's theirs es suyo
them: it's them son ellos/ellas
  it's for them es para ellos/ellas
  give it to them déselo
then entonces
  (after) después
there allí
  there is/are ... hay ...
  is/are there ...? ¿hay ...?
Thermos flask ® el termo
these: these men estos hombres
  these women estas mujeres
  these are mine éstos son míos
they ellos/ellas
thick grueso
thin delgado
think pensar
  I think so creo que sí
  I'll think about it lo pensaré
third tercero
thirsty: I'm thirsty tengo sed
this: this one éste/ésta
  this man este hombre
  this woman esta mujer
  what's this? ¿qué es esto?
  this is Mr ... éste es el señor ...
those: those men esos hombres
  those women esas mujeres
throat la garganta

throat pastilles las pastillas para la garganta
through por
thunderstorm la tormenta
ticket *(train etc)* el billete
  (theatre etc) la entrada
ticket office la taquilla
tide la marea
tie *(noun)* la corbata
  (verb) atar
tight ajustado
tights los pantis
time tiempo
  what's the time? ¿qué hora es?
timetable el horario
tin la lata
  (material) hojalata
tin-opener el abrelatas
tip *(money)* la propina
  (end) la punta
tired cansado
tissues los kleenex ®
to: to England a Inglaterra
  to the station a la estación
  to the doctor al médico
toast la tostada
tobacco el tabaco
today hoy
together juntos
toilet el wáter
toilet paper el papel higiénico
tomato el tomate
tomato juice el zumo de tomate
tomorrow mañana
tongue la lengua
tonic la tónica
tonight esta noche
too *(also)* también
  (excessively) demasiado
tooth el diente
  back tooth la muela
toothache el dolor de muelas
toothbrush el cepillo de dientes
toothpaste la pasta dentífrica

torch la linterna
tour la excursión
tourist el/la turista
tourist office la oficina de turismo
towel la toalla
tower la torre
town la ciudad
town hall el ayuntamiento
toy el juguete
track suit el chandal
tractor el tractor
tradition la tradición
traffic el tráfico
traffic jam el atasco
traffic lights el semáforo
trailer el remolque
train el tren
trainers los zapatos de deporte
translate traducir
translator el traductor
  (female) la traductora
travel agency la agencia de viajes
traveller's cheque el cheque de viaje
tray la bandeja
tree el árbol
trousers los pantalones
true cierto
  it's true es verdad
try intentar
tunnel el túnel
tweezers las pinzas
typewriter la máquina de escribir
tyre el neumático

umbrella el paraguas
uncle el tío
under ... debajo de ...
underground el metro
underpants los calzoncillos
underskirt la combinación
understand entender
  I don't understand no entiendo
underwear la ropa interior

United States Estados Unidos
university la universidad
unleaded sin plomo
until hasta
unusual poco común
up arriba
  (upwards) hacia arriba
urgent urgente
us: it's us somos nosotros/nosotras
  it's for us es para nosotros/nosotras
  give it to us dénoslo
use *(noun)* el uso
  (verb) usar
  it's no use no sirve de nada
useful útil
usual corriente
usually en general

vacancies *(rooms)* habitaciones libres
vacuum cleaner la aspiradora
valley el valle
valve la válvula
vanilla la vainilla
vase el jarrón
veal la (carne de) ternera
vegetables la verdura
vegetarian vegetariano
vehicle el vehículo
very muy
  very much mucho
vest la camiseta
video *(tape)* la cinta de vídeo
  (film) el vídeo
video recorder el (aparato de) vídeo
view la vista
viewfinder el visor de imagen
villa el chalet
village el pueblo
vinegar el vinagre
violin el violín
visit *(noun)* la visita

(verb) visitar
visitor el/la visitante
vitamin tablets las vitaminas
vodka el vodka
voice la voz

wait esperar
  wait! ¡espere!
waiter el camarero
  waiter! ¡camarero!
waiting room la sala de espera
waitress la camarera
  waitress! ¡señorita!
Wales Gales
walk *(noun: stroll)* el paseo
  (verb) andar
  to go for a walk ir de paseo
walkman ® el walkman ®
wall la pared
  (outside) el muro
wallet la cartera
war la guerra
wardrobe el armario
warm caliente
  (weather) caluroso
was estaba/era
washer la zapatilla
washing powder el detergente
washing-up liquid el lavavajillas
wasp la avispa
watch *(noun)* el reloj
  (verb) mirar
water el agua
waterfall la cascada
water heater el calentador (de agua)
wave *(noun)* la ola
  (verb) agitar
wavy *(hair)* ondulado
we nosotros/nosotras
weather el tiempo
wedding la boda
week la semana
welcome *(verb)* dar la bienvenida
  you're welcome no hay de qué

143

wellingtons las botas de agua
Welsh galés
Welshman el galés
Welshwoman la galesa
were: we were éramos/estábamos
  you were era/estaba
  (familiar) eras/estabas
  they were eran/estaban
west el oeste
wet mojado
what? ¿qué?
wheel la rueda
wheelchair la silla de ruedas
when? ¿cuándo?
where? ¿dónde?
whether si
which? ¿cuál?
whisky el whisky
white blanco
who? ¿quién?
why? ¿por qué?
wide ancho
  3 metres wide de tres metros de anchura
wife la mujer
wind el viento
window la ventana
wine el vino
wine merchant el vinatero
wing el ala
with con
without sin
woman la mujer

wood *(material)* la madera
wool la lana
word la palabra
work *(noun)* el trabajo
  (verb) trabajar
worse peor
worst (el) peor
wrapping paper el papel de envolver
  (for presents) el papel de regalo
wrist la muñeca
writing paper el papel de escribir
wrong equivocado

year el año
yellow amarillo
yes sí
yesterday ayer
yet todavía
  not yet todavía no
yoghurt el yogur
you usted
  (familiar) tú
your: your book su libro
  (familiar) tu libro
  your shoes sus zapatos
  (familiar) tus zapatos
yours: is this yours? ¿es suyo esto?
  (familiar) ¿es tuyo esto?
youth hostel el albergue juvenil

zip la cremallera
zoo el zoo